W
Xmas
Cynthia,
Collins, CO

THE GOOD, THE BAD, AND THE UGLY
DENVER BRONCOS

THE GOOD, THE BAD, AND THE UGLY
DENVER BRONCOS

HEART-POUNDING, JAW-DROPPING, AND GUT-WRENCHING
MOMENTS FROM DENVER BRONCOS HISTORY

Adrian Dater

TRIUMPH
BOOKS

Library of Congress Cataloging-in-Publication Data

Dater, Adrian.
    The good, the bad, and the ugly Denver Broncos / Adrian Dater.
        p. cm.
    Includes bibliographical references.
    ISBN-13: 978-1-57243-975-7
    ISBN-10: 1-57243-975-0
        1. Denver Broncos (Football team). I. Title. II. Title: Denver Broncos

GV956.D37D38 2007
796.332'640978883—dc22

                                                                    2007014875

This book is available in quantity at special discounts for your group or organization. For further information, contact:

Triumph Books
542 South Dearborn Street
Suite 750
Chicago, Illinois 60605
(312) 939-3330
Fax (312) 663-3557

Printed in U.S.A.
ISBN-13: 978-1-57243-975-7
Design by Patricia Frey
All photos courtesy of AP/Wide World Photos unless otherwise indicated.

CONTENTS

FOREWORD

My career in professional football certainly had its share of wonderful moments before I came to Denver in 1970. I won a Super Bowl the year before, playing with Joe Namath and the New York Jets. I kicked three field goals in our 16–7 victory over the Baltimore Colts in Miami. I remember like it was yesterday, watching Joe trot off the field with his right index finger waving in the warm air.

I played in the famous "Heidi" game with the Jets in 1968. This was the game where I kicked a field goal to give us a 32–29 lead with 1:05 left in the fourth quarter. After the kick, NBC went to a commercial. When they came back, viewers didn't see the last 65 seconds. They saw the movie *Heidi,* starting at its regularly scheduled time. Maybe that was a good thing for all those angry Jets fans that flooded the NBC switchboards, though; the Raiders scored 14 points in that last minute and beat us.

I was on the cover of *Sports Illustrated,* got to experience going through the streets of New York in a ticker-tape parade, and got to play in a pioneering league, the AFL, which helped change the sport forever.

But right up there, with all those great things, are the nine years I spent with the Denver Broncos. There was no ticker-tape parade for me there, no Super Bowl rings, or *Sports Illustrated* covers. There were some tough times, to be sure; some bad football at times, with plenty of frustration. But, man, there were some unbelievably great times, too. I got to be on the first Broncos team that ever went to a Super Bowl in 1977. I got to really experience what "Orange Madness" was all about in that wonderful year. I got to really experience what it was like in Mile High Stadium to have 80,000 people yelling and stomping their feet for you. Let me tell you, I still get chills just thinking about that.

Denver Broncos fans are like no other. I can't tell you how passionate they are for their team. How many fans out there have loved their teams so much they were willing to paint their house in funky colors, as many in Denver did in my day? How many orange-and-blue houses have you seen in your neighborhoods? In Denver, they were commonplace. I could have moved my family anywhere after my career ended in 1979, but there was never any doubt we'd continue to make our home in Denver. The natural beauty of Colorado, and the passion people have for life there, is infectious. That is especially true of their love for the Broncos.

This book, by longtime Denver sportswriter Adrian Dater, nicely chronicles the Broncos' history—of its humble rise from AFL laughingstock to being one of only three teams in National Football League history to play in six Super Bowls. There have been so many great football players who have worn the Orange and Blue, and I had the great fortune to do so as well. I played with many of the players whose stories are told in this book, and I've been just as big a fan of many of the ones who played for the Broncos after I left.

It is with the greatest of pride when I look up and see my name beside so many others in the Broncos Ring of Fame. And it is also with great pride that I can introduce this collection of stories to what I know will be many thousands of Broncos fans still to come.

— Jim Turner

ACKNOWLEDGMENTS

I t takes a village to build a book, and this space is dedicated to the villagers who helped build this one.

Thanks to the many players and other NFL personnel who agreed to be interviewed and are quoted in the text, with special thanks to Marlin Briscoe, Jim Turner, Frank Tripucka, Charley Johnson, Billy Thompson, Mark Schlereth, and Rich Karlis for their additional time and insights.

Thanks to the editors at *The Denver Post*, particularly sports editor Scott Monserud, for allowing the book to be written, along with use of their archives for research.

A special thank you to Broncos vice president of public relations, Jim Saccomano, for his help in locating many former players and coaches and for his additional insights.

Thanks to the following insightful and fine books that greatly helped the compilation of this one: *Tales from the Broncos* by Floyd Little and Tom Mackie, *John Elway: Armed and Dangerous* by Clay Latimer, *Denver Broncos: Colorful Tales of the Orange and Blue* by Larry Zimmer, and the Broncos' 2006 media guide. Thanks to the *Rocky Mountain News*'s Kevin Vaughn for an insightful 2000 article on Mile High Stadium called "Toast of the Town." Thanks to NFL Films for some source material, including quotes and sound bites from the 1987 AFC Championship Game and others pertaining to Broncos history.

Along with the several newspapers and websites mentioned in the text, the following websites were also very helpful: www.pro-football-reference.com, www.profootballhof.com, and www.youtube.com.

Thanks to others whose insights contributed to the text, including Mark Kiszla, Sandy Clough, Terry Frei, Reggie Rivers, Gary Miller, Jim Armstrong, Mike Klis, and Bill Williamson.

As always, thanks to my wife, Heidi, and son, Thomas Alan Michael, for letting me disappear for hours at a time with the phone and computer.

THE GOOD

MILE HIGH STADIUM: A MILLION MEMORIES

Everybody thinks of the late Mile High Stadium as just a place where football was played, and why not? The Denver Broncos were its main tenant for 41 years, with a bucking white Bronco statue adorning its entrance.

Not many people today know that Mile High Stadium was first called Bears Stadium, and its construction was hoped to be the catalyst to lure a Major League Baseball team to Denver—not a football team.

In 1947, Bob Howsam, his father, Lee, and his brother, Earl, purchased the Denver Bears, a minor league baseball team in the old Western League, for $75,000. The Bears played at a field called Merchants Park, but its decrepit condition made it imperative a new stadium be built. Denver mayor Ben Stapleton—who would later have the city's airport named for him—promised a sweetheart deal to the Howsams if they transformed the site of the city dump, just east of Federal Boulevard. The Howsams were all for it—$1 for 15 acres of land—but Stapleton lost his reelection bid and incoming mayor Quigg Newton, according to reports at the time, charged the Howsams $33,000 for the land.

Bob Howsam, who would later go on to be president of the Cincinnati Reds in their "Big Red Machine" days from 1967 to 1977, wanted desperately to bring big-league baseball to the

Rockies, but he continually had his ambitions thwarted for one reason or another.

But on August 14, 1948, Bears Stadium officially opened, with the Howsam family putting themselves deeply in debt to help finance it. Most sports owners then weren't the mega-rich individuals or corporations of today that look at their teams as toys. For families like the Howsams, the teams were their main business, and they sweated out all the finances.

The Bears beat the Sioux City Soos 9–5 in the first-ever sporting event at Bears Stadium, drawing nearly 11,000 fans. Throughout the 1950s, the Bears were a minor league affiliate for the New York Yankees, baseball's most glamorous franchise.

But the Howsams never could persuade a big-league team to move to Denver, and in 1959 the family looked toward landing a pro football team. The powerful NFL, however, did not want a team in Denver. So the Howsams bought into the fledgling American Football League and set up shop in 1960.

In the process, Bears Stadium was expanded into 34,657 seats, with 8,100 coming in the form of the South Stands and another 9,616 on the east side. While the newly named Broncos were a loser their early years, the team became a part of the city's fabric. People loved to go to big Bears Stadium and watch the giant men run around the field, trying to knock each other's blocks off.

Still, the Howsams mostly joined the AFL—a venture everybody said was doomed—to make Bears Stadium and the city of Denver more attractive for a major league baseball team. The football team was supposed to be the "other" tenant, to pro baseball.

But Howsam's dream of big-league baseball in Denver never came to fruition. Saddled with debt and seeing no hope of a pro baseball team coming anytime soon, in 1961 the Howsams decided to sell both the Broncos and the Bears. For a short time, it seemed certain the teams would move to San Antonio, as a solid offer was on the table from a group there. But two Denver businessmen, Calvin Kunz and Gerald Phipps, came to the rescue and bought the teams. They would both be staying in Denver, and seven years later, Bears Stadium was given a facelift—a new,

Denver's Mile High Stadium was host to many memorable Broncos games, teams, and players through the years.

16,000-seat upper deck. By 1968, more than 50,000 people could fit comfortably into the stadium, and it was in that year that the name was officially changed from Bears Stadium to Mile High Stadium.

From the start of the 1970 NFL season, after the Broncos had successfully merged from the AFL, no ticket ever went unsold at Mile High for the Broncos. That included the additional tickets from yet another facelift for Mile High: in 1974, city voters agreed to fund a $25 million expansion that would bring the number of seats to 75,100 by 1977. A massive top deck was added, which seemed to kiss the clouds.

The stadium's final capacity, after 60 penthouse suites were constructed in 1986, was 76,098. One of the stadium's most unique features was its east stands, which were movable thanks to a thin sheet of propelled water. In essence, the east stands were

TOP 10

John Elway's Favorite Touchdown Passing Targets

1. 42—Shannon Sharpe
2. 35—Vance Johnson
3. 23—Ed McCaffrey
4. 21—Mark Jackson
5. 21—Anthony Miller
6. 19—Rod Smith
7. 16—Steve Watson
8. 10—Steve Sewell
9. 9—Butch Johnson
10. 8—Clarence Kay, Clint Sampson, Michael Young

floatable, and they were moved to accommodate added field size for a baseball game.

What the stadium really became known for to the rest of the country was its noise. The extremely high seat decks bottled up noise better than today's more airy structures. When Broncos fans were yelling at the tops of their lungs and stomping their feet—as they frequently did—true Rocky Mountain "thunder" seemed to emanate.

"There will never be a football stadium as loud as Mile High," former kicker Rich Karlis said. "I don't care what anybody says; it was louder in there than anyplace I've ever been."

In 1993, Major League Baseball finally came to Denver, and appropriately enough the expansion Colorado Rockies played at Mile High. Massive, sellout crowds were the norm at the former dump site, for both Rockies and Broncos games. That same year, Pope John Paul II visited Mile High on World Youth Day. It was probably the stadium's most memorable year, but another near decade of memories was yet to come.

Included was a tribute night to a retired John Elway, the 1998 AFC Championship Game, and countless big-name rock concerts such as the Rolling Stones and U2.

But time started to take a heavy toll on the stadium's rusted beams, and by the end of the century fans were complaining about a lack of restroom facilities, less-than-easy access up and down from seats, and inadequate parking. After a lengthy fight with the city over financing issues, the Broncos built Invesco Field and began play there in 2001. Some fans—and even, for a while, *The Denver Post*—refused to acknowledge the field's new corporate name, still calling it "Mile High Stadium."

4

In March of the next year, the wrecking ball finally came to the old stadium. It hit some longtime fans hard, but by the coming years, most players and fans appreciated the new stadium—while never forgetting the old one.

"Every time I drive by where it used to stand, I can't help but think of Mile High and all that happened there, to me and my life, but also so many other people in this city," former Broncos cornerback Billy Thompson said. "I think it really helped give Denver an identity. For years, when people said 'Denver,' they also said, 'Oh, yeah, where Mile High Stadium is.' It was a sad time for me when they tore it down, but nothing lasts forever and the new stadium [Invesco Field at Mile High] is beautiful."

THE FIRST TWO WEEKS: THIS GAME IS EASY

When the Broncos play these days, whichever TV station carrying the game routinely gets ratings nearing 70–80 percent of the total Denver viewing audience. Home games are automatic sellouts, and pretty much every daily newspaper in the state sends reporters to cover them. Prior to the Broncos' first-ever game on September 9, 1960, however, you had to look hard in the Denver newspapers for any mention of the team. Three days before the game between the Broncos and the Boston Patriots—the first not only in Broncos history but also of the American Football League—this was the headline on the third page of *The Denver Post*'s sports section: "Broncos Drill for Loop Debut." Hardly a big buildup. *Post* Broncos beat writer Bob Bowie began his short story thusly, with a dateline of Los Angeles: "Denver's wandering Broncos head for the East again this week, but this time play for keeps. Friday night, they have the honor of opening the new American Football League campaign against the Boston Patriots in the Hub City.... Coach Frank Filchock is not pleased with the prospects of the long haul to Boston, but he's grooming for it, nonetheless. 'It's going to be a real good league,' [Filchock] said, 'and we'll be all right, too.'"

The first Broncos team had training camp in Pomona, California, and went 0–5 in the preseason, including a 43–6 loss to the Patriots, coached by a man who would walk the Mile High Stadium sidelines a few years later, Lou Saban. The preseason loss to the Patriots on August 5 was the first game of any kind the Broncos ever played. The first AFL game was played at Boston University, later named Nickerson Field. A stiff breeze greeted the players, as did 21,597 paying fans. The Patriots were installed as 16-point favorites by the wise guys in Las Vegas.

The Broncos began the week in Pomona, stopped in Denver for a Wednesday practice at Bears Stadium, then flew to Boston later that night. The Patriots had been home all week, waiting for their vertical-stripe-socked opponents. The Broncos got in late to Boston, sleeping away much of Thursday, and bused over to the small, primitive college football field to make history. The massacre that many thought would happen to the Broncos in Boston didn't; Denver, on the strength of a 76-yard punt return for a touchdown by Gene Mingo in the third quarter, beat the Patriots 13–10.

"Johnny Unitas and Big Daddy Lipscomb rose off the sandlots to football immortality with the Baltimore Colts. Friday night Gene Mingo, Denver Broncos halfback, started in that direction as he led the underdog Westerners to a 13–10 upset of the Boston Patriots as the American Football League became a reality after more than a year of planning," Bowie wrote in the *Post*. "The swift 21-year-old Negro from Akron, Ohio—who never played college football—dazzled 21,597 cash customers."

"I remember the wind that night," Broncos quarterback Frank Tripucka recalled. "That's why I only passed the ball [15 times, completing 10]. It was real dark. The lights weren't any good in that place. But I just remember walking into the locker room thinking 'We're 1–0.'"

Broncos general manager Dean Griffing exulted in the victory, telling Bowie later that night, "Denver will be in the playoffs." Austin "Goose" Gonsoulin preserved the victory with a last-minute interception—one of two picks he made against Pats QB Butch Songin. But the real hero was the aforementioned Mingo. He scored the winning touchdown and kicked the extra point on Denver's first-ever touchdown, a 59-yard pass from Tripucka to receiver Al Carmichael. That, of course, doubled as the first AFL TD in league history. "That's something I'm proud of," Tripucka said. "I remember the pass. It was a little swing pass, and [Carmichael] made the play. But Gene's punt return was what won us the game. It just seemed to come out of nowhere. But it really fired up the boys."

The Broncos did not return to Denver to a hero's welcome. Unlike the modern era—where teams fly back home the night of a game—the Broncos stayed on the East Coast in preparation

TOP 10

Most 100-Yard Rushing Games in Broncos Regular-Season History

1. 11—Terrell Davis, 1998
2. 10—Clinton Portis, 2003
3. 10—Terrell Davis, 1997
4. 8—Clinton Portis, 2002
5. 7—Terrell Davis, 1996
6. 7—Otis Armstrong, 1974
7. 6—Reuben Droughns, 2004
8. 6—Mike Anderson, 2000
9. 5—Gaston Green, 1991
10. 5—Bobby Humphrey, 1989

for their second game, in Buffalo. But the team didn't practice in Boston or upstate New York. Partly to offset costs, they practiced at the high school field on which Tripucka played, in his hometown of Plainfield, New Jersey.

The Buffalo Bills were not supposed to be a great team, but this was their home opener at War Memorial Stadium, and Denver again entered as an underdog. The team's record when the game was over, however, was 2–0, atop the AFL's Western Division. The Broncos won 27–21, with Gonsoulin emerging with four interceptions against Bills QB Tommy O'Connell. Defensive back Johnny Pyeatt's 40-yard interception return for a touchdown was the winning play.

"We have no one real star on this team—everyone pulls together," *Post* writer Bowie quoted Filchock to begin his story. "Coach Frank Filchock's defensive unit turned the tide for the Rocky Mountain boys, much to the dismay of 15,229 patrons in War Memorial Stadium." About Gonsoulin, Bowie wrote, "The light-fingered, 22-year-old defensive cop, ran his season's total to six with Sunday's thefts."

This game was easy. The Broncos might never lose. Bring on the next victim. That was the mood in the locker room as the team took its act downstate to face the New York Titans.

Despite getting 25 first downs to New York's 17, despite 413 yards of total Denver offense to 279 for the Titans, New York prevailed 28–24. New York won in miraculous fashion, blocking a punt by Denver's George Herring with 15 seconds left, with Filchock electing to punt on fourth-and-eight from the Denver 25-yard line. Center Mike Nichols snapped the ball at the feet of Herring, who scooped it up and tried to kick it away. Titans defender Nick Mumley blocked the kick, and teammate Roger Donahoe picked it up at the 12 and rumbled into the end zone as time ran out.

TRIVIA

Which team did the Broncos defeat for their first-ever playoff victory?

Find the answers on pages 175–176.

"The shabby orange letters on the Eighth Avenue side of the Polo Grounds, hard by the crummy Harlem River, proclaim simply: N.Y. Giants," Bowie began his recap for the *Post*. "They are faded nostalgic reminders of the halcyon days here at the foot of Coogan's Bluff. But, after what transpired Friday evening on the threadbare turf, the ramshackle old joint proved it's still one of our better thrill palaces."

One simply executed punt and the Broncos would have returned to Denver as a 3–0 AFL powerhouse. That it didn't happen, in the wake of the last-minute gaffe in New York, made for a tougher flight back to Colorado for the Broncos. Still, if anybody had told Tripucka beforehand his team would be 2–1 after the first three games on the road, he would have been happy.

"The loss to the Titans was a big disappointment, but we did feel good about what we did," he said. "We ended up winning the first home game [against Oakland], and if we'd been 4–0 by then, I really think we'd have made the playoffs. I think we would have been on such a high, that we would have made it. But that blocked punt hurt. That's the one thing that went wrong on that whole first road trip, but it cost us a game."

FRANK TRIPUCKA: THE ACCIDENTAL QUARTERBACK

The first quarterback in Denver Broncos history was never supposed to have played for the team.

Frank Tripucka in 1960 was a 32-year-old man who had just finished his seventh season playing quarterback in the Canadian Football League, with Saskatchewan and Ottawa. Prior to that, he played five forgettable seasons in the National Football League with three teams. The last one, the Dallas Texans in 1952, was a nightmare for Tripucka. He was part of a team that went 1–11, and he threw 17 interceptions in his six games, with only three touchdown passes.

Tripucka, an All-American at Notre Dame, thought his football career was finished as the new decade dawned. He had played 11 years of professional football; time to move on and do something else.

"I thought, 'I'm an old man now,'" Tripucka said.

Being a coach intrigued the native of Plainfield, New Jersey, so it was with considerable interest that Tripucka accepted Frank Filchock's invitation to help coach the fledgling Denver Broncos of the new American Football League.

Filchock, hired by the Broncos as head coach, had held the same job for several years in Saskatchewan, with Tripucka as his QB. He thought Tripucka would be just the man to help develop whoever might emerge as his Broncos quarterback.

"We had our first camp in Golden, at the Colorado School of Mines," Tripucka said. "I'd only been to Colorado one other time, for an exhibition game with the Chicago Cardinals."

It quickly became apparent to Filchock that he had little talent to choose from in his pool of quarterback hopefuls. So, with the season fast approaching, Filchock approached Tripucka with a proposition: would he give playing one more year a shot?

"My career in the NFL didn't end so well, so part of me wanted to try and redeem myself," Tripucka said. "But I was obviously a little apprehensive."

Tripucka signed on as a player. It turned out the "old man" had some good football still left in him. Three good years, in fact. In the 1960 AFL season, Tripucka completed 248 of 478 passes for

THE SNOW BOWL

Probably the best thing to happen for the up-and-down Colorado economy of the 1980s was a *Monday Night Football* game on October 15, 1984, at Mile High Stadium. That night the entire country witnessed a game between the Broncos and Green Bay Packers played in an absolute blizzard. The Packers fumbled on their first two possessions from scrimmage, leading to Denver touchdowns. But the game came down to the right foot of kicker Rich Karlis—a right foot that was bare. Somehow, Karlis avoided frostbite and kicked the winning field goal in a 17–14 Denver victory. The game proved a boon for the Colorado ski industry, as thousands of people from around the country saw the snow and booked winter ski vacations.

3,038 yards and 24 touchdowns. His passing yardage, attempts, and completions led the league, and his touchdowns tied for second.

"There are so many memories from that first year in Denver," Tripucka said. "We started the season out East. Our first three games were on the road, and we won two of them."

Indeed, the newly minted Broncos couldn't play at home until week 4 because Bears Stadium in Denver was occupied by the Bears minor league baseball team.

Tripucka led Denver to a win in its first-ever game, the 13–10 triumph over the Boston Patriots on September 9, 1960. Coming home with a 2–1 record, the Broncos were greeted with a parade down 16th Street in Denver. To call it a parade might be a generous use of the word, however; few people actually showed up, many with "Who are these guys?" looks on their faces.

The first home game, on October 2, saw 18,372 people in the stands. That might have been a generous number, too.

"[Receiver] Lionel Taylor would always say, 'We outnumbered the fans' in that first year," Tripucka said. "It was pretty empty at times, but they were still good fans. They could make some noise."

The Broncos won that first home game, 31–14, over the Oakland Raiders. After six games, they were a gaudy 4–2, with visions of the playoffs starting to dance in their heads. But the team would not win another game that season. It was not Tripucka's fault, however.

He continued to pile up the points and passing yards, but the Broncos' defense was porous, especially its run defense. While Tripucka helped Denver have more passing yards than opponents in the 1960 season, the Broncos allowed nearly twice as many rushing yards as they gained (2,145 to 1,195).

Tripucka re-signed with Denver for the 1961 season, but things didn't go as well for him or the team. His passing yardage dropped to 1,690 and his touchdown passes to 10. The team went just 3–11 and his friend and coach, Filchock, was fired.

"Frank was a good man, but he hated coaching," Tripucka said. "He didn't like things like playbooks and meetings. He would just as soon go out and play touch football."

Filchock was replaced by Jack Faulkner, previously a backfield coach with the San Diego Chargers. Faulkner had a more organized coaching mind, particularly when it came to offense. He told Tripucka to let 'er rip throwing the ball, and the old man QB didn't disappoint. He led the AFL again in passing yards (2,917) and threw for 17 touchdowns. Taylor was always his favorite target, with Taylor catching a league-high 77 passes.

The 1962 Broncos were riding high at 6–1 midway through the season, when the wheels fell off again.

The defense, which had been good to that point, became sievelike again. The team lost its last five games, including a 46–45 heartbreaker to the New York Titans in front of 15,776 fans on November 22 at Bears Stadium.

"We could have made the playoffs that year, but it didn't work out," Tripucka said. "We didn't play well down the stretch, and I include myself in that."

Tripucka came back for the 1963 season, but by now he was 35 and finally starting to show some age. He played just two games, completing 7 of 15 passes for 31 yards. It became clear that it was finally time to hang up his cleats.

Tripucka went on to be a head coach in the CFL and then settled into a life in private business, buying a plastics manufacturing company. He fathered six boys and one daughter. His son, Kelly, starred in basketball for Notre Dame and played 10 years in the NBA. Today, he maintains an office at his Central Plastics firm in New Jersey and is a doting grandfather.

He still watches Broncos games regularly. In fact, the day after an October 9, 2006, *Monday Night Football* Broncos win over the Baltimore Ravens, when talking to the author, Tripucka referred to the Broncos as "we" and basked in the victory.

His No. 18 remains one of only three jerseys retired by the Broncos, and his name is enshrined at Invesco Field at Mile High on the Ring of Fame.

"It's a great honor, something I'm very proud of and humbled by," he said.

MARLIN BRISCOE: FIRST BLACK QUARTERBACK

From the day the United States was founded, racism has been an unfortunate blend of its fabric. Perhaps no year in the 20th century was as racially charged as 1968.

There were the assassinations of civil rights leaders Martin Luther King and Robert F. Kennedy, subsequent race riots in many big cities, and the rise of the Black Power movement at that year's Summer Olympic Games.

In those many ways, progress toward racial harmony and equality was set back in 1968. But that year did see a landmark development in racial equality come to professional football: for the first time in history, a black man started a game at quarterback for a pro team, and his name was Marlin Briscoe.

A skinny, 5'11", 178-pound native of Oakland, California, Briscoe was drafted by the Broncos in the 14th round of the 1968 draft after he starred at quarterback at the University of Nebraska–Omaha. Briscoe set 22 school records at Omaha as a quarterback and was named All-America.

Briscoe had been a quarterback at every level of his football life, and he had every intention of continuing at the position with the American Football League Broncos. But Broncos coach Lou Saban had vastly different ideas. He told Briscoe the only way he could make the team was as a cornerback. The perception among those in power in pro football was that, for whatever reasons, blacks did not make good quarterbacks. The unspoken but implied rationale was that blacks were "athletes" only, without the cerebral necessities to make it at a "thinking man's" position.

Briscoe knew it was hogwash, and he entered Broncos training camp with a stipulation in his contract that he be given a three-day tryout for the quarterback position. In front of fans and media, Briscoe dazzled in camp, outperforming the seven other quarterback hopefuls in front of him on the team's depth chart—despite not getting as many repetitions as the others. The media took notice, suggesting that Briscoe be the starter for the season.

Still, Saban began the season with veteran Steve Tensi, who had never completed more than 41 percent of his passes in a season and who did not account for a single offensive touchdown in Denver's last three preseason and first two regular-season games. In week three, against the Boston Patriots at Mile High Stadium, Tensi was having another dismal performance when he suffered a broken collarbone.

The fans wanted Briscoe, and Saban reluctantly agreed to make him his new QB. With his team down 20–10, Briscoe nearly led the

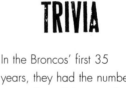

TRIVIA

In the Broncos' first 35 years, they had the number one rushing defense in the league three times. What were those years?

Find the answers on pages 175–176.

Broncos to victory before falling 20–17. The next week, against the Cincinnati Bengals, Briscoe made history by becoming the first black man to start at quarterback. He led Denver to a 10–7 victory, and in week 5 he led the Broncos to a shocking 21–13 road victory over Joe Namath and the mighty New York Jets.

A black man could succeed at quarterback, Briscoe showed. He made smart decisions in the pocket and read defenses astonishingly well for a rookie. He would finish the 1968 season with 1,589 yards passing in only 11 games, with 14 touchdown passes—still a Broncos rookie record. He beat the Miami Dolphins and star quarterback Bob Griese with a late 10-yard sneak up the middle in week 7, and he piled up huge numbers in wins over Boston and Buffalo.

If it wasn't for the Broncos' porous defense that season, Denver's final record of 5–9 could have easily been reversed thanks largely to Briscoe's play.

"I thought I had done a lot to prove the naysayers wrong about me and the black quarterback in general," Briscoe said. "Forgetting that I was black, they also always used my size against me that I couldn't be a good QB in pro football, but you couldn't argue with the results."

It was a shock, therefore, when Briscoe, back at Omaha in the off-season finishing up his degree, "heard through the grapevine" that Saban was holding team quarterback meetings—without him. Briscoe hopped a plane to Denver and stood silently outside one of the meetings, waiting to confront Saban.

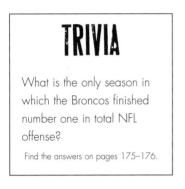

TRIVIA

What is the only season in which the Broncos finished number one in total NFL offense?

Find the answers on pages 175–176.

"He couldn't even look me in the eye," Briscoe recalled. "To this day, I've never gotten a reason why I wasn't given a chance to be the quarterback the next season."

For the 1969 season, Saban went back to Tensi, who led Denver to a 5–8–1 season. In training camp, realizing he wasn't getting a shot to keep the QB job he felt he'd earned, Briscoe asked for his release. He soon signed with the Buffalo Bills, but Briscoe was not given the chance to play quarterback there, either.

Reluctantly, he agreed to play a position he had never played before—wide receiver—and would go on to a successful rest of his nine-year career, catching passes, not throwing them. He led the AFC with 57 receptions for Buffalo in 1970, earning Pro Bowl honors, and was a regular player on Miami's Super Bowl champion teams in 1972 and 1973. Ironically, it was Saban who, as the new coach in Buffalo, traded the former 14th-round pick Briscoe to Miami in 1972—for their number one pick in the draft in 1973, who turned out to be Joe DeLamielleure. Briscoe finished his career with the New England Patriots in 1976.

The director of a boys and girls club in Long Beach, California, today, Briscoe looks back proudly on his one, groundbreaking year in Denver. Sometimes referred to as the "Jackie Robinson of Pro Football," Briscoe's story was turned into a feature film titled *The First Black Quarterback*, with a book on his life by the same name published in 2002. He still is received warmly by fans in Denver when he returns every year for an alumni reunion, and he has been honored by some of the black quarterbacks whose careers might not have been possible if not for Briscoe's persistence. When Warren Moon was inducted into the Football Hall of Fame in 2006, he thanked Briscoe in his acceptance speech.

TOP FIVE

Records of NFL Teams, 1983–98

1. San Francisco—192–62–1 (.755)
2. Denver—161–93–1 (.633)
3. Miami—154–101–0 (.604)
4. Washington—144–110–1 (.567)
5. Chicago—143–112–0 (.561)

There is a "what if" factor in Briscoe's speech, however, when he looks back on his career.

"I had a lot of good things happen in my career. Two Super Bowl rings, a receiving title, things like that," he said. "But I do wonder what I might have been able to do if I'd just been given the chance to keep playing quarterback. A quarterback is always how I've thought of myself as a football player."

FLOYD LITTLE: THE FIRST BIG STAR

Before Floyd Little was drafted by the Broncos in 1967, a reporter approached the 5'10", 195-pound Syracuse running back and made a bad joke with a bad pun.

"You're just a 'Little' guy, aren't you," Little recounted in his semiautobiographical book.

Ha ha. Funny guy. "Little" did the reporter know that Floyd Little would go on to become one of the NFL's best running backs. Little did the reporter know Floyd Little had the certified, psychologically tested personality of a homicidal maniac.

"My heart is as big as any man out there," Little told the reporter, thankfully not ripping his head off.

Floyd Little did have a big heart, but he was much more than just one of those guys with a Napoleon complex and not enough talent.

"Floyd had as much natural ability as anyone in the game at that time," former Broncos teammate Billy Thompson said. "He had great speed; I mean, he was fast. But more than that, he knew how to play the game and was a smart player. There just wasn't a lot around him. That's not a knock on the guys that played with him offensively, but it's just a fact."

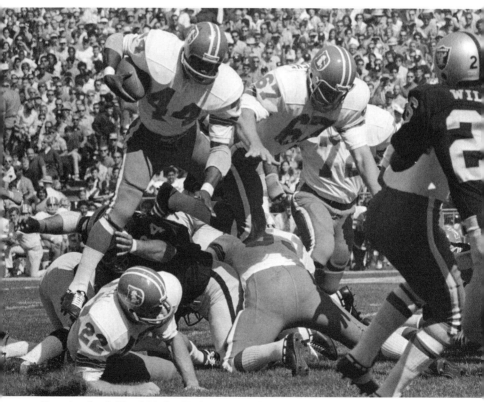

Running back Floyd Little climbs over a pile of players during a 1970 game against the Raiders. (Photo courtesy of Bettmann/Corbis)

Floyd Little was a superb player on a lot of bad teams, and that was the great misfortune of his career. Lots of excellent players played on mediocre teams in their careers, never winning a championship. But few, if any, had that bother them more than the native of New Haven, Connecticut.

Little came out of Syracuse in 1967 believing he would play for his favorite team, the New York Jets. Coach Weeb Ewbank told him he would be taken with the number 12 pick in the first merged NFL draft, and Little looked forward to a career playing with Joe Namath, in front of his Eastern friends and family.

But then *Sports Illustrated* came out with a preview issue that said Little would not be a great pro because of his size, and his stock seemingly began to slip. Back then, with no round-the-clock sports media, no Internet, and football a blip on the national consciousness compared to today, things like a bad write-up in *SI* mattered. A lot.

Pro sports drafts back in those days were held entirely over the phone. Decision makers from every team would listen through tinny speakers as the commissioner told them it was their turn "on the clock." All they had to go by in selecting their players were, if they were lucky enough to have seen them, their own scouting reports. Teams actually would call sports reporters from high school or college newspapers, asking for an opinion on a player they might want but had never actually seen in person. Sometimes, the reporter's opinion would carry the day in a team selecting or not selecting a player.

Sports Illustrated's downgrade of Little, despite his outstanding career at Syracuse University—where he wore the same number, 44, as the legendary Jim Brown—worried the Orangeman star to no end. He would not even be drafted, he thought. After all, Brian Piccolo went undrafted two years before, and he led the nation in rushing and scoring for Wake Forest.

But Little's fears were unfounded. He was tabbed by the Broncos with the sixth overall pick. He had never been west of the Mississippi, but Little came to love the beauty of the Rocky Mountains right away.

Little went on to have a great career, finishing as the seventh all-time leading NFL runner when he retired in 1975, with 6,323 yards and 54 touchdowns. He became the first Bronco to win an AFC rushing title, with his 901 yards in 1970. In '71, on a team that finished 4–9–1, Little led the entire NFL with 1,133 yards. From 1968 to 1973, in fact, no player in the NFL gained more yards from scrimmage, either on the ground or through the air, than Little.

But Little never got to run in a playoff game. The high number of wins for any Broncos team he ever played for was seven (twice). Only in the last couple of years of his career did the Broncos start to have some good talent around him offensively, with players such as Otis Armstrong, Haven Moses, Riley Odoms, and Charley Johnson. But by then, injuries from the constant hitting from years of being the Broncos' only real threat with the football, had taken a heavy toll.

By 1974, he had a bad knee and ran for just 117 carries that year, averaging 2.7 yards per run. He gutted it out for one more season, but the final game of his career, in Miami, was spent on the sideline, after he twisted an ankle in the second quarter.

But his final home game, December 14, 1975, against Philadelphia, was one from the Hollywood scripts. Little, who announced he would retire after the season, scored two touchdowns in the victory, including a 66-yarder after catching a screen pass. By game's end, Little broke down in tears. The man who didn't know a thing about the city of Denver when he was drafted, who always dreamed of being a Jet, had an orange and blue heart. He loved the team, the city, and its fans. They loved him back.

When the clock hit all zeroes, Little was carried off the field—by two fans.

Two brawny but everyday Broncos fans lifted Little up and gave him the sendoff every player can only dream about.

"That was the single greatest moment of my career and it came at the very end," Little wrote in his memoirs. "To be carried off the field by the greatest fans in the world in my last game at Mile High Stadium is something I'll cherish until the day I die."

That Little's most memorable moment, for him, did not happen in a game illustrates the depth of mediocrity of his Broncos teams. But ask any Broncos fan who went to games then, and they'll tell you they have a warm list of memories, mostly provided by the small man with the big heart.

CHARLEY JOHNSON: THE PROFESSOR

A few players in pro sports have been nicknamed "the Professor," either for the way they might look or their IQ or both. Charley Johnson, who quarterbacked the Broncos to their first two winning seasons, is a real-life professor at a major university.

Browse through the New Mexico State University's rostrum of classes and you'll see Dr. Charley Johnson, professor of chemical engineering. It's the same Johnson who helped find the winning formula for the first time in Broncos history, in 1973, when Denver finished 7–5–2.

"We took a lot of pride in having that first winning season," Johnson recalls. "To us, that was quite an accomplishment, and it still feels good to be able to say it."

Charley Johnson was supposed to be a washed-up, broken-down barge of a QB when the Broncos gave up a third-round draft pick to the Houston Oilers in 1972 for him. Johnson had just come off two serious injuries that required surgery, to a knee and shoulder. The Broncos just hoped Johnson might be a nice, veteran backup to their hotshot young prospect, Steve Ramsey.

Johnson wound up stealing Ramsey's job and today has his name on the Broncos' Ring of Fame—despite playing with the team for only four years—1972–75.

"I certainly didn't expect that," Johnson said. "But, it's definitely a great honor from Pat Bowlen."

Johnson admits he "sneaks a peek" at his name every time he returns to Invesco Field at Mile High, which is usually once a year for the Broncos' annual Alumni Day. When he arrived in Denver in 1972, Johnson was just hoping to get his name back up high on an NFL depth chart. He threw only 94 passes for the Oilers in 1971, playing second fiddle to rookie Dan Pastorini.

"I thought my career was over, basically," Johnson said.

But new Broncos coach John Ralston thought the former New Mexico State Aggie might have a little more good football in him. Johnson played the good soldier in the first five games of the '72 season, wearing the traditional baseball clip and holding a clipboard while serving as Ramsey's backup.

The Broncos were 1–4 in those games, however, and in week 6, just prior to his 34th birthday, Johnson was given the start in Oakland against a Raiders team that would finish 10–3–1. Johnson turned back the clock, to his early years when he was an All-Pro with the St. Louis Cardinals. In front of 53,551 black-and-silver fans at Oakland–Alameda County Coliseum, Johnson was the star in the Broncos' shocking 30–23 victory—the Raiders' only loss at home that season.

TOP FIVE

All-Time Rushing Quarterbacks
(entering 2007)

1. Randall Cunningham—4,928
2. Steve Young—4,239
3. Fran Tarkenton—3,674
4. Steve McNair—3,570
5. John Elway—3,407

Johnson started every game the rest of the season and had some great moments, including the final two games in which the Broncos scored 83 points in wins over San Diego and New England. Unfortunately, the Broncos defense still wasn't very good, and Johnson finished 4–5 as a starter after replacing Ramsey.

Many pundits predicted Ramsey would win back his job the following year, but it didn't happen. Johnson started all 14 games in 1973 and had an excellent season. He threw for 2,465 yards—third in the NFL—and 20 touchdowns. In a 48–20 win against his old team, Houston, Johnson became the 18th QB in NFL history to throw for 20,000 yards.

If a bounce or two had gone Denver's way, especially in their two tie games against Oakland and St. Louis, the Broncos would have had a good shot at making the playoffs for the first time. But in those days, only four teams from each conference qualified for the postseason, and Denver finished tied for second in the AFC West with Kansas City at 7–5–2. A tough 21–17 loss at Oakland closed out Denver's season, but there was still a lot of satisfaction in the organization at finally having a winning season.

The prospects for 1974 looked great, especially with the addition of rookie standout linebacker Randy Gradishar from Ohio State and sophomore running back Otis Armstrong, who showed flashes of stardom the year before. Plus, there were still names such as Floyd Little, Haven Moses, and Riley Odoms for the old warhorse Johnson to work with.

The '74 season got off to a bad start, however, at 0–2–1—including a 30–3 loss in Washington in week 3. Some fans started calling for Ramsey to return as starter, but Ralston stuck with Johnson and things started to turn around. Johnson led the Broncos to another exciting win in Oakland in week 11, then racked up big offensive numbers in subsequent wins over Detroit and Houston. But Johnson got hurt prior to the final game, at San Diego, and Ramsey was awful in a 17–0 Denver loss to a bad Chargers team that ended any hopes for a playoff spot, the Broncos season ending at 7–6–1.

At age 36, Johnson came back for another year in 1975 and again beat out Ramsey for the starting job. The season started off with a bang, including a thrilling opening day, 37–33 victory over the Chiefs at Mile High Stadium. That was followed by a win over Green Bay, and everybody thought this would be the year the Broncos finally made the playoffs.

But things started going badly. Denver lost five of its next six games, and after a 26–13 loss to the Chiefs in week 6, Johnson lost his starting job to Ramsey. Johnson would never start another game for the Broncos, seeing little duty the rest of the way on a team that finished a highly disappointing 6–8.

"I really respected John Ralston as a man and football coach," Johnson said. "But I think he was sensitive to criticism that he didn't know his offense very well. But he didn't need to know that offense. I think he started thinking he had to show people he did, though, and started doing a lot more of the play-calling. It wasn't very good."

The last year could have gone better, but Johnson calls the four years he spent in Denver, out of the 15 he spent in the NFL, "some of the best ever."

He said he still receives "three or four letters or packages a week" asking for autographs of Broncos memorabilia. In addition to serving on the faculty at NMSU, Johnson serves as the assistant to the president for athletic progress at the school.

"It's great. I get to have it both ways, teaching chemical engineering to kids and still talking football with the players and coaches," Johnson said. "I'm a lucky guy."

RICK UPCHURCH: MR. EXCITEMENT

Before there was a Billy "White Shoes" Johnson or a "Neon" Deion Sanders—flashy players known for their electrifying punt or kickoff returns—there was Rick Upchurch.

In the 1970s, there was no better return man than the native of Toledo, Ohio, who grew up raised mostly by his grandfather, Louis, until he died when Rick was in high school.

"We always stood on the sidelines and watched when Ricky had a chance to touch the football," teammate Billy Thompson said. "He set up so many short-field situations for our team. He was a real weapon for us."

In his prime with the Broncos—including 1977, Denver's first Super Bowl team—Upchurch might have been the most popular player on the team. And, if not the best player, he was in the top three.

Upchurch had dazzling, evasive running skills. In 1976, He ran four punts back for touchdowns, averaging a league-leading 13.7 yards per return, including a 92-yard TD. In '77, he ran a punt back 87 yards for a TD, and a 75-yarder the year after that. A four-time Pro Bowl player, it was shocking that Upchurch still wasn't a Broncos Ring of Fame member entering 2007. Upchurch's 3,008 career punt-return yards is still, far and away, the Broncos record. While Floyd Little (16.88, in 1967) still holds the team record for punt-return yard average in a season, Upchurch has the next three highest averages.

In Super Bowl XII against Dallas in 1978, Upchurch returned a kickoff 67 yards—a Super Bowl record at the time—that set up the touchdown that temporarily got the Broncos back in the game in the third quarter.

Five years later, he was still at the top of his craft. In 1982, he had one of his best years, averaging 16.1 yards per punt return, with two more touchdowns.

"He was the best at returning kicks, and a great guy," kicker Rich Karlis said. Upchurch didn't just return kicks, however. In fact, he holds the distinction of being the first NFL player to catch a pass from John Elway, in 1983—Upchurch's final year. He had excellent hands, as well as feet, catching 40 passes that final year and a team-leading, career-high 64 in 1979.

Upchurch had compact, muscular legs that made him extremely difficult to take down with just one hit. He often bounced off would-be tacklers until he found a little open space—and then he was off to the races. Often, punt returns are a time for fans to stretch their legs, maybe grab a bite at the concession stand. In Denver, in the Upchurch years, punt returns were an event, not to be missed.

Upchurch was the 1975 NFL Rookie of the Year—the first Broncos player to win the award. Upon his retirement, he held or co-owned seven NFL punt-return records, including being the leading yardage return man in league history.

But, like many Denver players before and after Upchurch, he never seemed to get his deserved, lifelong recognition. He was selected to the all-time, First-75-Year NFL Team, as picked by the Pro Football Hall of Fame's selection committee. But, perhaps because he failed to play 10 years—he finished with nine—enshrinement into the Hall has eluded him.

Upchurch today is a happily married father of four, but in his single days around Denver he dated Condoleezza Rice—who went on to become U.S. secretary of state.

He always had a soft spot for kids, always a champion of the underdog-type kid he was. In 2005, he took a job as coach of East High in Pueblo, Colorado. In football-crazy Pueblo, Upchurch still is like a rock star, signing dozens of autographs after games.

1977: A CRUSH ON THE ORANGE

It is almost impossible to impress upon younger people just how big the Broncos were to Coloradans in the winter of 1977. "Broncomania" was no gross exaggeration, no gimmicky media tag. Webster's defines *mania* as "excitement of psychotic proportions accompanied by disorganized behavior and mood." Does painting one's house orange and blue count as excitement at a psychotic level?

"The first time I saw someone's house painted orange in Denver, I really couldn't believe it," said Jim Turner, the Broncos' place-kicker from 1971 to 1979. "I mean, that's somebody's *house*. That's where they live. To love your team so much to do something like that, I mean, that's Broncomania right there. The fans were always great in Denver before that, but things really went to a whole new level that year."

Said cornerback Billy Thompson, captain of the '77 Broncos: "I'll give you an example of how crazy it was that year. The night we beat Oakland [to win the AFC Championship], there was an orange arrow from the middle of the intersection near my house, all the way to my garage door. There were oranges in my mailbox, there was orange toilet paper all over my trees. People were honking at me on the highway all the way home. They knew what kind of car I had."

In the playoff run that culminated with the team's first Super Bowl appearance, on January 15, 1978, Santa Claus dressed in orange in many Denver stores. Local department store Fred Schmid had "orange tag" sales, not red. People had orange Christmas trees, orange-tinted garage lights, orange cars, and you can imagine what the number one soft drink in the Mile High City was at that time. Fanta, the Coca-Cola subsidiary that had long produced a soda called "Orange Crush" saw its sales increase more than 10,000 percent in Denver. Stores could not keep cans on the shelves any longer than the time it took to put them there. "I still have some cans of it in my basement," Thompson said. "They made a commemorative can just for the Broncos. It was something else."

The 1977 Denver Broncos were a team with a new coach, Red Miller. A former Broncos assistant, Miller replaced John Ralston following 1976, in which Ralston led Denver to a 9–5 record, the best mark in team history to that point. Ralston, also the team's general manager, rubbed some veterans the wrong way, however, with a collegiate, sis-boom-bah atmosphere. More than a few players thought Ralston was just too corn-ball for the pro game—with one of his traditions a Saturday night "ice-cream social" that made players' eyes roll. He also was known for long, grueling training-camp practices—not helped by the fact that Ralston decided to move camp to the hot, smoggy campus of Cal Poly Pomona.

When it became clear he had lost too many players, Ralston resigned and Miller was hired on February 1, 1977. With his orange hair and creased, mountain-man face, Miller had the right look to coach a Broncos team, at least. But could he really coach?

TRIVIA

John Elway played more years in a Denver uniform than any other player in Broncos history (16). Who are the two players tied for second?

Find the answers on pages 175–176.

"Yes," said Thompson, who today works in community relations with the Broncos. "Red was a players' coach. He treated players like men, though, which made you want to play hard for him. Ralston was a different kind of guy. He was kind of out of the Dale Carnegie school—power or positive thinking type."

But kicker Turner, never at a loss for words, said Ralston has not been given enough credit for Denver's first Super Bowl team.

"That team was built by John Ralston. That was really his team, his guys," Turner said. "But, that's not a knock on Red, either. He was a good coach for us. He helped us get to the next level, but that was John's personnel."

The Broncos won their first six games, but the win streak was stopped in week 7 by the Raiders at Mile High Stadium. The defending Super Bowl champion Raiders were favored to beat the Broncos, either in the AFC West or in a playoff matchup should one come about. The Broncos had beaten the Raiders 30–7 earlier in the season, in Oakland, with Denver linebacker Tom Jackson famously yelling "It's all over, fat man" at Raiders coach John

Linebacker Tom Jackson (57) and lineman Lyle Alzado (77) spearheaded Denver's defense known as the "Orange Crush" during their Super Bowl run in 1977. (Photo courtesy of Getty Images)

Madden following a fumble recovery. But the Raiders' win in the rematch at Mile High Stadium just two weeks later reiterated pundits' belief that the best team in the AFC still wore silver and black—not orange and blue.

Broncos fans could be forgiven for having an inferiority complex to the Raiders then; Denver still had never even been to a playoff game, while teams like the Raiders, Dolphins, and Steelers had been recent champions in the AFC.

But there just seemed to be something about the 1977 Broncos. For one thing, the team had a ferocious, helmet-flying, hard-hitting defense. Thompson, Randy Gradishar, Lyle Alzado, Tom Jackson, Barney Chavous, Louis Wright, Steve Foley, Rubin Carter, and Bob Swenson all would become household names in Denver before long, part of a defense dubbed the "Orange Crush."

The Orange Crush defense held teams to 10 or fewer points in seven of the Broncos' 14 games that season. The only game in which they gave up more than 14 points was the 24–14 loss to Oakland at Mile High. The defense allowed an average of just 109.4 yards rushing per game and had 25 interceptions to opponents' 12, with 37 sacks. Defensive coach Joe Collier had instituted a 3–4 defense prior to the season, partly because of an injury to the colorful Alzado, and by '77 Denver's linebackers made Collier's scheme look masterful.

Gradishar, the middle linebacker, was a truly great player and team leader—who continues to be slighted from the Pro Football Hall of Fame for some strange reason.

"If Randy Gradishar didn't play in Denver, he'd be in the Hall of Fame by now," said Thompson. "In the history of the Denver Broncos [entering 2007] there is only one player in the Hall of Fame [John Elway]. How is that? There have been so many great players on our teams."

The Broncos won the division, finishing one game ahead of the Raiders, and on December 24, 1977, the first playoff game in Broncos history took place, against the 1976 Super Bowl champion Pittsburgh Steelers. Terry Bradshaw, Franco Harris, Mean Joe Greene, Jack Lambert, and company flew to Denver intent on showing that the "Orange Crush" was a fraud. Pittsburgh had a "mediocre" 9–5 season, but this was still Terry Bradshaw and the Steelers here. Was the "Orange Crush" really a better defense than the "Steel Curtain?"

In the fourth quarter, the answer was still uncertain. When Bradshaw threw a one-yard TD pass at the 1:42 mark of the fourth quarter, the score was Broncos 21, Steelers 21. It was a tense time in Mile High. Could this first-time playoff team really beat the veteran Steelers in the clutch?

Yes. Turner's 44-yard field goal, with 11:31 left in the game, would prove to be the winning play. But the Broncos would tack on 10 more points for good measure. The Broncos intercepted Bradshaw three times, with Tom Jackson getting two.

Meanwhile, the Raiders won an epic playoff game in Baltimore that same day, to set up an AFC West title showdown in Mile High on New Year's Day.

It would turn out to be one of the better playoff games in NFL history. The crowd was incredibly loud, and the play on both sides was superb.

Fans in Denver swear Mile High was never louder than when, in short succession, Swenson intercepted Raiders star QB Ken Stabler to the Oakland 14, and quarterback Craig Morton—who was so sore he had to have Red Miller tie his shoelaces before the game—threw a 12-yard TD pass to receiver Haven Moses, with 1:29 gone in the fourth quarter. That made the score 20–10 Broncos, and everybody had one thing in mind at that point: Super Bowl.

Not so fast. The Raiders had one last champion's punch in them. The left-handed, bearded Stabler hit tight end Dave Casper with a 17-yard touchdown pass with 3:16 left in the fourth, cutting the Denver lead to three points.

Those last minutes were a combination of nail-biting anxiety and get-out-of-your-seat-and-roar time for Broncos fans. The Broncos had the NFL's number one rushing defense that season, and Oakland finished with just 94 yards on 36 carries (2.6 average). But nobody wanted to see the ball in Stabler's hands again with a chance to tie or win.

They didn't. The Broncos got the ball back with 3:08 left and never let it go. Wide receiver Moses had a career, Ring-of-Fame

"THE BOZ" AND BIFF BATTLE

Some of the most entertaining Broncos games of the 1980s came against the division rival Seattle Seahawks—particularly when Seattle drafted a brash, outspoken linebacker from Oklahoma named Brian Bosworth in 1987. Bosworth was beloved by reporters for his many colorful comments, not to mention his wild, blond Mohawk. "The Boz" was a national sensation coming out of college, winning the Dick Butkus Award, and turned into a good NFL player for a while. He made the All-NFL Rookie Team in 1987, after signing a 10-year, $11 million contract. Bosworth tried to get under the skin of Broncos QB John Elway with words or taunts, but it rarely worked. Elway had some big games against the Boz and the Seahawks, including a 40–17 whipping in Bosworth's first pro game, September 13, 1987. Fans at Mile High Stadium loved to get on Bosworth, many coming with homemade signs mocking his Mohawk and appearance in a cheesy action movie, Stone Cold, in which he starred. Bosworth's career flamed after three years because of a shoulder injury, but he provided some good theater to Broncos fans for a while.

day, catching five passes for a whopping 168 yards and two touchdowns.

"What I think about mostly when I think back to 1977 is the Raiders game," Thompson said. "It was a special game. That was the game that changed the history of the Broncos. After that game, it was expected, not only from the guys, but the fans, for the organization to be successful. Fans poured onto the field, tore the goal posts down. That didn't happen much in the pros." The Broncos, that former team with the goofy socks and foolish white belts, were going to Super Bowl XII in New Orleans.

"Do they believe in us now?" Jackson shouted in the locker room afterward. "Do they believe in us NOW?"

"By now, it's time to savor, and enjoy, and let yourselves get a little giddy," longtime *Denver Post* columnist Dick Connor wrote. "Eighteen years on the temperance wagon are long enough. Pour it down. The Denver Broncos, the clown princes of the old AFL, the court jesters, have seized control of the kingdom and toppled the king himself."

The next two weeks were a dizzying, unorganized, fun, but ultimately unfulfilled time for Broncos fans.

If they weren't making the trek to New Orleans, fans spent many hours organizing huge Super Bowl parties at home. The local supermarkets ran out of things like potato chips and buffalo wings, and liquor stores did some of their most intense business in Colorado's colorful alcohol-fueled history. Everybody—everybody—in Colorado geared up for the big game, at the New Orleans Superdome. The opponent would be the Dallas Cowboys—America's Team—led by legendary quarterback Roger Staubach and a rookie running back from Pittsburgh named Tony Dorsett. Defensively, the Cowboys had names such as Harvey Martin, Randy White, Cliff Harris, Ed "Too Tall" Jones, Thomas "Hollywood" Henderson, and D.D. Lewis.

TRIVIA

Name the first four players inducted to the Broncos' Ring of Fame, in 1984.

Find the answers on pages 175–176.

The Broncos did not receive the kind of posh accommodations one expects for today's modern sports teams. They stayed at a run-down Sheraton near the Superdome. One night running back Otis Armstrong was sent scampering from his room because of a big, Bayou cockroach. The team practiced at decrepit Tulane Stadium, while the Cowboys received more modern accommodations on and off the field.

The magical run of '77 ended on January 15, 1978. The Cowboys won, 27–10. White and Martin—named co-MVPs—hounded the hobbled Morton around the backfield all day, forcing four interceptions. Morton was lifted for backup Norris Weese, who directed a scoring drive that cut the lead to 20–10. But, on a halfback option, Cowboys back Robert Newhouse hit receiver Golden Richards with a 29-yard TD pass to put the game out of reach.

The difference in the game was the Cowboys defensive line and the turnover department. The Broncos forced six fumbles by the Cowboys but recovered only two. Denver fumbled four times and lost all four. That, on top of Morton's four interceptions, was way too many turnovers to give a team like Dallas.

Broncomaniacs in the stands did not collapse in their seats and weep. They gave their orange men one last, long cheer and generally partied the last night away in the French Quarter. Sure, it would have been great to win. But the Broncos had so many firsts that season, and such a fun ride to New Orleans, that a funereal mood was impossible.

"We'll be back," they chanted.

"There's no use crying on anybody's shoulder," Broncos defensive end Barney Chavous told longtime *Denver Post* columnist Dick Connor. "We lost. But we have the coaches and ability to correct that."

They wouldn't return to the Super Bowl for another nine years. "I think of a sense of accomplishment, when looking back on the Super Bowl," Thompson says today. "Defensively, we were ranked first in the AFC and third in the NFL. We knew our defense had to play a major role. We played pretty well, I think, but they were a great team. We just came up a little short, but I'll never forget the high-fives and slaps on the back we got from our fans when the game was over. That's the kind of thing that has kept me a Denver Bronco for life."

TOM JACKSON: MR. COLORFUL

Turn on ESPN during the football season and chances are Tom Jackson will be on the screen, gesticulating with his hands, speaking rapid-fire into the camera.

Jackson, who played more seasons for the Broncos than any other player except John Elway, moved faster on the football field in his 14 NFL seasons—all with Denver. The Cleveland native has always seemed to have the perfect life, but there was pain with the glory. In 1997, Jackson lost a daughter, Andrea, age nine, in a car accident. He lost his mother as a teenager, his father shortly after. Physically, he has a hard time walking now, the pain of arthritis too much to bear at times. The 14 years of all-out sacrifice of his body catches up with him when it's time to get out of bed in the morning. But there is nothing Jackson would trade from his football career. Winning a Super Bowl would have been nice, of course, but the man who wore No. 57 has had an envious life.

Jackson is another in the long line of Broncos stars who wasn't given much of a chance coming out of high school or college. Although he was a star linebacker at Cleveland's John Adams High, Jackson was told, at 5'11", he was too small to play for his dream school of Ohio State. After nobody else in the Big 10 would give him a scholarship, Jackson accepted one from the University of Louisville. The Cardinals were a floundering program—long gone were the glory days when Johnny Unitas played for the school—but coach Lee Corso turned things around with fresh recruits like Jackson.

The Cardinals went 9–1 in 1972, and Jackson finished his career there a two-time Missouri Valley Conference Player of the Year. Jackson thought he might be drafted in the first round of the 1973 NFL Draft, but his name still hadn't been called after the first three. "By the time the third round went by, I considered not playing football," Jackson told the Louisville *Courier-Journal*. "I was so angry that I could have played the way I played and not have been drafted by that time."

The Broncos finally selected Jackson in the fourth round, but most NFL experts thought Jackson still too small to make an impact. But Jackson would be one of the first players to break the mold of what a linebacker was supposed to be; he proved you didn't have to be oversized to be an effective defender, up close to the line. He got to runners faster than anybody more often than not, and he was a great tackler.

"I don't think there was anybody faster on the football field than T.J.," said former Broncos quarterback Charley Johnson.

"You could tell, when he was a rookie, how bad he wanted to succeed. He had a fire for the game and for life."

Jackson started only four games in his rookie season, but he made a positive impact on the club's first-ever winning season (7–5–2). The Broncos lowered their points allowed from 350 to 296, with Jackson contributing 31 tackles, 26 of them unassisted.

The next year, Jackson established himself as the leader of the defense. He led the 7–6–1 team with 121 tackles, including four sacks. By 1977, Jackson was a star.

He made the first of three consecutive Pro Bowls and was the best defensive player on the field in Denver's first-ever playoff victory, 34–21 over Pittsburgh on Christmas Eve. Jackson intercepted two Terry Bradshaw passes and recovered a fumble at the Pittsburgh 10-yard line that led to Otis Armstrong's TD run on the next play, giving Denver a 14–7 lead.

Jackson had another strong game in Denver's AFC title win over Oakland and was the best defensive player wearing orange in Super Bowl XXII against Dallas. He led the Broncos with seven tackles, sacked Cowboys Hall of Fame QB Roger Staubach, and recovered a Cowboys fumble. But the Cowboys defensive line was just too much, in their 27–10 victory.

Ten years later, Jackson would start in another Super Bowl—becoming the first Bronco to do so. He was still a tremendous player, and he was the unquestioned team leader in the locker room. His verbal abilities made him a powerful motivator to teammates, and he was always sought out by reporters for his comments.

It was after Denver's 39–20 loss to the New York Giants in Super Bowl XXI, however, that Jackson thought of life after football. He knew he was a good talker and thought maybe he could parlay a playing career into one in the broadcast booth.

In 1985, ESPN began a weekly football preview show, hosted by Chris Berman. Jackson was a fan, and he wondered if the network could use an ex-player like himself to complement the show. While he probably could have played another year or two with the Broncos, Jackson decided to give a career in TV as big an effort as he did as a player. ESPN was impressed with what it saw, and in 1987 Jackson joined Berman on the set. He has been there ever since. In 1992, Jackson was the only Bronco selected to the Ring of Fame. Jackson was never shy about expressing his opinions as a player, and he certainly wasn't shy on the set. There were a couple of brushes with controversy for Jackson, including being called a profanity by Patriots coach Bill Belichick following a Super Bowl win, after Jackson had said none of Belichick's players could stand him. He wondered on air if fellow ESPN analyst Michael Irvin was "retarded" following some comments he made about the Manning football family (Jackson quickly apologized). He also caught some flak for not speaking out more against Rush Limbaugh, following comments the conservative commentator made about black Eagles quarterback Donovan McNabb during his brief tenure with ESPN.

But that is a pretty skimpy docket of controversy for the first 20 years of a broadcast career. Otherwise, anybody who spends any amount of time with Jackson seems to come away thinking of themselves as a friend of "T.J."

"He's a great guy, and was a better teammate," said former Broncos kicker, Rich Karlis.

JOHN ELWAY: THE LEGENDARY NO. 7

He was called the "Duke of Denver," as much a nickname of homage to the grit and heroism of John Wayne in the movies to actual royalty. John Elway is as close to being the King of Denver as any historical figure, real or imagined.

Nearly a decade after his retirement from the Broncos, Elway's No. 7 jerseys were still an everyday sight in Denver. So were his several car dealerships. And his popular restaurant. And the indoor football team he owned. And his charity foundation, and his annual golf tournament, and several other business endeavors.

All were wildly successful, just like Elway's long career with the Broncos, from 1983 to 1998. If anybody seemed to have the perfect life and career, it is Elway—but it wasn't always so. There was a time in Denver when Elway was known as the quarterback who couldn't win the Big One. He took the Broncos to three Super

BY THE NUMBERS

1984–92—John Elway averaged 3,172.6 yards passing per season in those first years of his career, with an average of 16.8 touchdown passes and 15.8 interceptions.

1993–98—Elway got better with age. In these last years of his career, he averaged 3,543.2 yards passing per season, with 23.7 touchdowns and 11.5 interceptions.

Bowls in his first nine seasons, but he was blown out in each one. Entering his 15th NFL season in 1997, Elway was a 37-year-old quarterback with an armful of individual awards, but no ring on his finger. He seemed destined to join the purgatory of great pro athletes—Ernie Banks, Charles Barkley, Dan Marino, Karl Malone—who never won a championship.

But it all changed on a gorgeous January Sunday afternoon in San Diego in 1998, in Super Bowl XXXII. In particular, it changed on one third-down play in the third quarter against the heavily favored, defending champion Green Bay Packers. On the Packers' 10-yard line, facing a third-and-six play in a 17–17 game, Elway scrambled out of the pocket. With bad knees having taken the sprinter's speed he once possessed, Elway lumbered toward the goal line. At about the 5-yard line, he leaped forward but was crushed by two Packers defenders, sending him spinning in air like a helicopter's rotor blade. Despite spinning a full 360 degrees from a violent, second hit from LeRoy Butler, Elway not only still had the ball in his hand, but he had the first down as well. Elway jumped to his feet and threw his fist in the air, his trademark big, buck teeth seemingly filling the stadium with their shine.

"I knew we were going to win that game right there," said his offensive lineman teammate, Mark Schlereth. "That just totally uplifted our football team so much, to see how bad John wanted it, with his bad knees and 37 years old. I tell people that it's all because of me, too, that if I'd just made my block, that play never would have happened." (Schlereth actually did not miss a block, but it makes for a good story anyway.)

The Broncos did win Super Bowl XXXII, 31–24. When linebacker John Mobley broke up Brett Favre's fourth-down pass with time running out, Elway leaped onto the field, his arms raised, his eyes showing a mixture of jubilation and seeming disbelief that he would, finally, hold the Vince Lombardi Trophy high.

When Broncos owner Pat Bowlen was first given the trophy, he wasted little time in handing it off to Elway, proclaiming, "This one's for John."

John Elway, acquired from a trade with Baltimore, is as much a Denver icon as the Rocky Mountains.

Elway would finish his career a champion again, winning the MVP award in Denver's 34–19, 1999 Super Bowl victory over the Atlanta Falcons and his old coach, Dan Reeves, with whom he previously feuded.

If Elway hadn't won any Super Bowls, he still would have been the first-ballot Hall of Famer he became in 2004. Even without the two championship rings, Elway's career feats were mind-boggling—especially considering he wasn't able to pass the football as much as he wanted under Reeves in his early years.

Among Elway's NFL records: 148 games won as a starting quarterback; 47 game-winning or game-tying drives in the fourth quarter; five-time Super Bowl starting QB; 50,000-plus passing yards and 3,000-plus rushing yards; seven consecutive 3,000-plus passing and 200-plus rushing yardage seasons.

He finished with 51,475 passing yards, second only to Marino on the all-time NFL list. Probably no quarterback in NFL history was as feared by opponents in high-pressure moments as Elway. His clutch reputation started to become legend in 1987, when he took the Broncos on a 98-yard, game-tying march up the field against the Cleveland Browns in the AFC championship game. "The Drive," as it would be memorialized, started with Denver down 20–13, with five and a half minutes left in the fourth quarter. Elway led the Broncos down the field in overtime, leading to Rich Karlis's game-winning field goal.

Elway might never have been a Bronco, for several reasons. The first was that the Baltimore Colts—not Denver—owned the first pick in the 1983 NFL Draft and made it no secret they would take Elway, who had just finished a great college career at Stanford. But Elway heard too many bad things about Colts coach Frank Kush and told the Colts he would not play for them if selected. He would pursue a career in baseball, he said, which at the time seemed a better choice. The New York Yankees had already signed Elway to a $150,000 bonus in his junior year at Stanford, and some people thought he would make a better baseball player than football player. Elway, in fact, played in the Yankees' minor league system after college, hitting .318 in a six-week stint with Oneonta (New York) of Double-A. Yankees owner

George Steinbrenner told *Sports Illustrated*, "I see a lot of Mickey Mantle in him."

At Stanford, Elway lived in a fraternity house, sleeping on a waterbed in a Spartan room that had just a couple of posters tacked on the wall. His frat brothers called him "Elwood" and weren't at all fazed by his celebrity. Elwood had to clean the toilets just like every other brother, even after signing a rich contract with the Broncos. That was fine by him; Elway hated star treatment, always preferring tipping back a couple of beers with his buddies over red-carpet media events.

TOP FIVE

Broncos Single-Season Reception Leaders

1. 113—Rod Smith, 2001
2. 101—Ed McCaffrey, 2000
3. 100—Rod Smith, 2000
4. 100—Lionel Taylor, 1961
5. 92—Lionel Taylor, 1960

Baltimore chose Elway anyway, but Elway held good on his promise not to report, and the Colts traded him to Denver for backup quarterback Mark Herrmann, the rights to tackle Chris Hinton (the number four pick in the draft), and a 1984 first-round pick. Even though Hinton ended up being a very good player, the trade would turn out to be the football equivalent of the Brinks Robbery.

To natives and visitors alike, Elway has become as associated with Colorado as the Rocky Mountains. If there were a Mount Rushmore in the Rockies, Elway's toothy grin no doubt would be one of the features chiseled into rock.

Today, he serves as co-owner and chief executive officer of the Colorado Crush of the Arena Football League, helping guide the team to the 2005 AFL title. He maintains an active presence in many Colorado business and charitable activities, and he still keeps a 1-handicap on the golf course. He briefly considered trying for his PGA Tour card, but he decided against putting in so many hours.

Already, Colorado football fans are salivating at the prospect of another Elway playing for the Broncos some day. In 2006,

Elway's son, Jack, was a quarterback on the state's perennial prep-school football powerhouse, Cherry Creek High School.

Jack's number? No. 7, of course. If he ever does play for the Broncos, he'll have to change it to another number. It's already been retired.

TERRELL DAVIS: THE DIFFERENCE MAKER

When he joined the NFL in 1995, as a sixth-round pick from the University of Georgia, Terrell Davis entered an era in which the influence of running backs was supposedly on the decline. Sure, there were great backs still in the NFL—Emmitt Smith and Barry Sanders among them. But it was the golden era of the "West Coast Offense" popularized by Bill Walsh with the San Francisco 49ers. Quarterbacks have been and probably always will be the most important players on a football team, but that seemed especially so in the mid-1990s. Along with Denver's John Elway, superstar QBs such as Jim Kelly, Dan Marino, Troy Aikman, Brett Favre, Steve Young, and Drew Bledsoe dominated their times. In football's earlier years, running the ball was the preferred choice of head coaches. Running backs—or defensive players that could stop the run—were often the difference makers for their teams. The Broncos had had fine running backs prior to Davis's arrival. Floyd Little, Otis Armstrong, Bobby Humphrey, and Sammy Winder all had excellent years with Denver. But entering the 1995 season, the Broncos' all-time single-season rushing record was Armstrong's 1,407, set in 1974. A terrific season, but that was still nearly 700 yards shy of the all-time NFL mark—2,105 yards by Eric Dickerson for the Los Angeles Rams in 1984. No Bronco had ever led the league in rushing since Armstrong.

All that would change in the next four years. Terrell Davis, overlooked in the first five rounds of the 1995 draft, would have arguably the greatest four-year "run" of any back in NFL history—culminating in two Super Bowl titles, 56 regular-season touchdowns, 6,413 yards on the ground, and a team-record 2,008 yards in a magical, almost perfect 1998 season.

"He was just so smooth and knew the offense so well," said offensive lineman Mark Schlereth, who opened many of the holes Davis would find in his short but brilliant career. "As time has gone on, I've just come to appreciate what he did so much more. We just didn't realize at the time how great this kid was and how much he really meant to us. But after he got hurt, in 1999, I think Olandis Gary came in and got about 1,200 yards. And we'd always say as offensive linemen, 'Well, that meant Terrell would have gotten 1,800' or when Mike Anderson had about 1,600 yards one year [actually 1,487], we'd say, 'That would have been 2,400 for Terrell.'"

Elway had been able to take the Broncos to three Super Bowls entering '95, but everybody knew how those turned out. Under Dan Reeves, the Broncos had always stressed a controlled, running approach to offense—but Elway had never had a truly dangerous running back to work with. New coach Mike Shanahan had a passing reputation upon his arrival, having been the former offensive coordinator of the 49ers, and he seemed to be gearing his Broncos toward a more diverse, passing attack. Receivers such as Anthony Miller and Rod Smith, along with tight end Shannon Sharpe, were seemingly higher priority weapons to Shanahan than any runners.

Davis changed all that. For reasons that not even he ever could adequately explain, the San Diego native—who began his college career at the now defunct University of California–Long Beach football program—became a completely different player once he hit the pros. His speed, good in college, became great in the NFL. So did his decision making, his toughness, and his confidence level. He ran for 1,117 yards his rookie season—sixth most in team history—and broke Armstrong's team record with 1,538 yards his second year. In 1997, he ran for 1,750 yards and was the MVP of Super Bowl XXXII in his hometown.

It is the '98 season, however, that Davis became otherworldly. He was incredible, not only leading the league with the 2,008 rushing yards and 21 touchdowns, but also becoming only the third runner in NFL history to run for more than 1,000 yards in a seven-game span. From September 7 through October 25, 1998,

Davis ran for 1,001 yards on 175 carries. Only Jim Brown (1,011, 1958) and O.J. Simpson twice (1,025, 1973; 1,005, 1975) gained more yards in as many games.

Because he was such a threat, Davis opened up the passing game for Elway. Defenses used to be able to focus just on Elway because they knew the Broncos didn't have a good enough

While Elway was unquestionably great, he didn't win a Super Bowl until Terrell Davis joined him in the Broncos backfield during their championship seasons. Here, Davis takes off on a 20-yard touchdown run against the Philadelphia Eagles during his epic 1998 season.

TOP FIVE

Longest Scoring Passes in Broncos History

1. 97—George Shaw to Jerry Tarr, at Boston, September 21, 1962
2. 96—Frank Tripucka to Al Frazier, at Buffalo, September 15, 1962
3. 95—Craig Morton to Steve Watson, vs. Detroit, October 11, 1981
4. 93—Craig Morton to Steve Watson, vs. San Diego, September 27, 1981
5. 90—Charley Johnson to Rick Upchurch, vs. Kansas City, September 21, 1975
t. 90—John McCormick to Bob Scarpitto, vs. Houston, October 17, 1965

running game, but, again, Davis changed everything. Elway, who loved to throw the ball and was frustrated all those years under Reeves when he couldn't, did not mind handing it off to Davis. Not when it could get him the elusive Super Bowl ring.

Through it all, Davis maintained a humility and likability increasingly rare for today's superstar athletes. He had a boyish grin and seemed to like to mix with reporters and fans.

After winning the Super Bowl MVP in San Diego, Davis signed a record nine-year, $56 million contract with the Broncos. He appeared on *The Late Show with David Letterman* and *Sesame Street* and saw the publication of his autobiography.

Many athletes have regressed after getting the big-money contract, but Davis made the deal look *cheap* in '98. It seemed nothing could slow down Davis entering 1999, but everything changed on an October day that year, at Mile High Stadium against the New York Jets. Trying to make a tackle following an interception, Davis's right knee buckled and twisted. He went down screaming, clutching the knee. A rut in the Mile High turf would eventually do what no defensive lineman ever could in the NFL. Three years of frustrating rehabilitations and aborted comebacks would follow. When the knee got better, enough to play in the 2000 season, Davis developed a stress fracture in a shin bone that took a long time to be detected on x-rays. For a while, some media, fans, and, incredibly, some of his old teammates, questioned Davis's toughness.

"That was ridiculous, because we knew what Terrell went through and we knew he had a lot of heart as a player," Schlereth said.

By the preseason of 2002, Davis just couldn't take it anymore. He retired after a Monday night exhibition game at home against San Francisco. During the game, when it became clear to him he couldn't perform at the level he was accustomed to anymore, Davis stood on the sideline and gave the fans one final salute—the one he'd done after so many touchdown runs.

Nearly 80,000 appreciative fans, some of them crying, saluted back.

ROD SMITH: RAGS TO RICHES

When he graduated from Missouri Southern State University in 1994, with degrees in three different business majors, Rod Smith was already one of the greatest players in NCAA Division II history. He was his league's all-time receiving yards leader (3,043) and touchdown leader (34) and a first-team All-American. The NFL's response was a collective yawn.

On NFL draft day, 1994, Smith's name went uncalled. Not one team thought enough of him to even take a flier with their last picks. What a loss for them, but not for the Broncos, who at least had the smarts to offer him a free-agent tryout the next year.

Thirteen years later, Smith was the leading receiver in Broncos history, in touchdowns, receiving yards, and total yards from scrimmage. He was the first undrafted player to ever surpass 10,000 receiving yards. He was the favorite deep threat of John Elway on Denver's first two Super Bowl–winning teams. His 113 receptions in 2001 is the all-time Broncos record.

Smith's draft-day humiliation might have been the best thing that ever happened to him. It fueled a burning rage, a drive to prove everyone had made a severe mistake by overlooking him. It made him never take anything for granted, to always work harder than the rest, even after enjoying instant NFL success.

How instant? Smith's first catch in the NFL, on September 17, 1995, was a 43-yard, game-winning touchdown grab against the Washington Redskins and All-Pro cornerback Darrell Green as time ran out on the clock. Not until two years later, however, did Smith definitively prove to the world he was a bona fide NFL star. In 1997, Smith caught 70 passes for 1,180 yards and 12 touchdowns. He did not catch a pass in Denver's Super Bowl victory over Green Bay, but he made up for that the following year, in Super Bowl XXIII in Miami.

Smith caught five passes in that game, for 152 yards, including an 80-yard TD bomb from Elway that started to put the game away for the Broncos, at 17–3 in the second quarter. Smith outran veteran Falcons defensive back Eugene Robinson to make the catch, the same Robinson who was arrested for soliciting a prostitute the night before and who disparaged the Broncos the previous year with the Packers, when he called them the "Indianapolis Colts."

Smith piled up one outstanding season after another following his great performance in Miami, but he often wore a scowl in those years. That's because nothing less than Super Bowl rings sufficed for him. He was the rare player who truly cared more about the team's success than his own. He held himself to the highest standard on the field and despised others who didn't do the same. He would not hesitate to publicly chastise a teammate he felt wasn't putting out 100 percent or who didn't want to win as much as he did.

He especially had it in for highly drafted players who didn't work hard enough or who he felt coasted by on their reputations. He never lost the scars from his own draft experience.

"People ask me, 'What did you think about the draft picks?' 'I said, 'Dude, I don't watch.' I'm still kind of bitter," Smith once told a Denver newspaper. "Some guys got drafted and they ain't played football in 15 years and I'm still waiting to get drafted. I'm still waiting to hear my name."

Smith posted 70 or more catches from 1997 to 2005, but he fell short of tying Tim Brown's all-time NFL record for most years in a row doing so when he slipped to 52 catches in 2006. Smith

Rod Smith makes a grab in front of Raiders safety Ray Buchanan in a 2004 game.

had excellent speed, but there were faster receivers in his day. He became a great player through endless, precise repetition of his routes and intense concentration on holding on to the football. His long, galloping stride put shorter defenders at a disadvantage once he caught the ball.

Smith was a leader in the community as well, serving as spokesman for the Broncos' annual blood drive. He easily identified with the underdog, donating lots of time and money to sick children. In 2004, he was a finalist for the Walter Payton Man of the Year award. The chip on his shoulder he had for the "silver spoons" in life, specifically in the NFL, was just as pronounced. That led to some outspoken moments with the media, including a few hilarious sound bites.

In 2005, the Broncos drafted former Ohio State runner Maurice Clarett in the third round. Clarett came out of college billed a potential superstar but with a controversial reputation for his attitude and work ethic. Not long into training camp, Clarett was sitting out with some minor injuries.

"You can't make the club if you're in the tub," Smith said. Clarett was cut from the club soon after.

In 2001, a receiver named Eddie Kennison fell into the doghouse of Broncos coach Mike Shanahan and later wound up with the rival Kansas City Chiefs. Kennison ripped Shanahan and the Broncos once he landed in KC, which didn't sit well with the fiercely competitive Smith. "This was pretty big talk from a guy that once quit the team 12 hours before kickoff eight weeks into the season," Smith told reporters. "He quit the night before a game. We were 4–4 and we needed him. I had to go out there and I had two rookies and a third-year guy playing receiver, and I'd rather go out there with some guys who wanted to play with their hearts."

Smith also loved to stick a verbal needle in the hearts of opposing fans, especially those of the Chiefs and Oakland Raiders. One year, the Hell's Angels–type Raiders fans were yelling profanities at Smith at the end of a big Broncos victory.

"Hey, if you leave now, you can beat traffic," Smith yelled back. Entering 2007, at age 37, Smith had no plans to quit. He needed 151 catches for 1,000, but more than anything, he wanted another chance at Super Bowl ring number three—the same number of his children. He is a lock to make the Pro Football Hall of Fame when he does retire. Not bad for a guy nobody wanted.

THE BAD

THE HALF-A-LOAF GAME

John Ralston, who coached the Broncos from 1972 to 1976, was sometimes disparaged for his pie-in-the-sky, rah-rah optimism. Lou Saban, who coached the Broncos from 1967 to 1971, was more of an old-school, browbeating type. But most of his players cared for him, went to battle for him.

Saban is remembered as a good coach who just didn't have very much talent—particularly at quarterback—in his Broncos years. Unfortunately for Saban, many older Broncos fans still remember him for the nickname, "Half-Loaf Saban."

Saban acquired the lamentable moniker because of some decisions in the final minutes of the 1971 season-opening game against the high-powered Miami Dolphins at Mile High. The Dolphins, who would go on to Super Bowl VI that season in New Orleans, had a star quarterback in Bob Griese, and a roster with other legendary names such as Paul Warfield, Larry Csonka, Larry Little, Mercury Morris, and Dick Anderson.

The Broncos were 5–8–1 the previous year and went into '71 with two new quarterbacks—Steve Ramsey and Don Horn. The team's best player was running back Floyd Little, but other than him, there was little offensive talent.

"Our whole offense was 'Floyd right, Floyd left, Floyd up the middle,'" said Broncos cornerback Billy Thompson.

IF ONLY...

Gary Kubiak had started the 1991 AFC championship game in Buffalo, instead of John Elway.

While it would have been considered treasonous to have started the backup Kubiak over the legendary Elway, the game's final statistics showed the outcome might have been different had Kubiak played all the way in the eventual 10–7 Broncos loss to the Buffalo Bills.

Elway had failed to move the Broncos all day against the Bills, when he was forced out of the game after three quarters with a leg injury and Denver down just 3–0. Kubiak completed 11 of 12 passes in the fourth quarter for 136 yards—15 more yards than Elway had in three quarters—and led an 85-yard touchdown drive that cut Buffalo's lead to 10–7 late in the game. Then, the Broncos' Steve Atwater recovered an onside kick at Denver's own 49, with 1:43 left and two timeouts. Kubiak hit Steve Sewell for seven yards on a first-down pass, but Denver's season was effectively ended when Bills cornerback Kirby Jackson stripped Sewell of the ball and Buffalo recovered.

The outcome also would have been different had Broncos kicker David Treadwell not missed three field goals, of 37, 42, and 47 yards.

An overflow crowd of 51,228—the largest in team history to that point—came to Mile High on September 19, 1971, to see the opener. The Dolphins were heavy favorites, with an offense that would finish second in NFL scoring that year. But with 2:30 left to play, the Broncos had a 10–3 lead on Miami. The defense, led by punishing lineman Paul Smith, was having one of its best games in years. Griese was intercepted by Charles Greer at the Broncos 1-yard line, but on their next possession, Griese tied the game for the Dolphins when he hit Warfield with a 31-yard TD pass.

The Broncos got the ball back but punted it to Miami with 1:20 left. Kicker Jim Turner, however, forced a fumble on the return with a hit on Jake Scott. When Bobby Anderson recovered for Denver, fans produced the roar that would come to character-ize football at Mile High. Denver had the ball in good field position with 1:14 left. Time to go for the winning score—or so one would have thought.

Instead, Saban made one of the most controversial and infamous coaching decisions in team history—then compounded the issue with a quote to the media that suggested he had not much faith in his team.

The Broncos' first three plays from scrimmage in the final drive were simple handoffs to Little, who finished with 70 yards on 23 carries. Where was the passing game? Wasn't it standard procedure for a team needing yards in a hurry to try to get them through the air? Only after Little ran for 11 yards on third down did Saban call for his first pass of the drive—and it netted 12 yards, a screen pass from Horn to Anderson. But on the next play, also an attempted pass, Denver was called for holding, pushing the ball back 10 yards and out of field-goal range.

Still, 15 seconds were left on the clock. Time for at least one more pass, where a good sideline throw could easily have gotten the Broncos close enough for a Turner field-goal attempt.

It didn't happen. Saban chose to send the ball up the middle to a tired Little, who was immediately hit at the line by a grateful Dolphins defense. With no timeouts left, the clock ran out, the game a tie (there was no overtime period in those days). The crowd went nuts—with boos. How could Saban be so conservative? they wondered. Where were the guts? Where was the Wild West, shoot-the-moon spirit?

"I remember standing on the sideline, waiting for Lou to send me in, waiting for him to come up to me. But he didn't. I was just like, 'hello?'" Turner said.

The Broncos locker room was library quiet. Players couldn't understand their coach's decision making. They wanted to go for it, of course, especially the hypercompetitive Little. As much as he wanted the ball in the big moments, he knew handoffs to him weren't the smartest play calls in a last-minute drive.

It was up to the Denver media to ask Saban for an explanation, and this was his quote: "I told [Horn] to stay on the ground until he got out where he had solid footing. It worked beautifully and if we don't drop the ball and get a holding penalty, we have

TOP 10

Most Broncos Fumbles in a
Season

1. 40—1961
2. 36—1984
3. 36—1996
4. 35—1979
5. 34—1988
6. 34—1983
7. 34—1963
8. 33—1999
9. 32—1960
10. 31—1991

the ball on their 30-yard line with a timeout remaining and a chance to get our field-goal unit into the game. But it didn't work out. It's an old saying, but I'd rather have half a loaf than none."

Saban thought a tie against one of the NFL's best would be good for his team's long-term morale. He thought it best to, in effect, be able to say, "We played the Miami Dolphins and didn't lose." But, to his players, it seemed to say, "I thought you guys might choke it away, so I ran out the clock."

The results of the following three weeks clearly suggest Saban's move backfired. Denver lost 34–13 the next game to a poor Green Bay team, then lost big the next two games, at home, against rivals Kansas City and Oakland. Fans booed Saban nonstop in those home games, with the media piling on. Everybody started calling him "Half-Loaf Saban" and many fans came to Mile High with literal half loaves of bread. Many were tossed onto the field, some striking players and coaches. None hit Saban, but the fans' action was symbolic; the coach was on the firing line, and after week nine—a 24–10 loss at home to the Bengals—Saban was gone.

"No question, that really hurt us, that first week, the half-a-loaf game," Turner said. "It hurt our morale, no question."

Saban quit before he could be fired. He officially resigned after the Bengals loss, the team's record at 2–6–1—with that "1" being the eyesore that fans just couldn't forget. Saban left without saying a word to his players, which rubbed many the wrong way. But Saban wasn't the weepy, emotional type, and he later said he felt too chastened to linger around. Better to just move on quickly.

Many Broncos fans wished he'd wanted to move just as quick on that fateful last drive against the Dolphins.

SUPER BOWL XXI: TOO MUCH SIMMS

The trilogy of terror that was the Broncos' three Super Bowl appearances, from 1987 to 1990, began on January 25, 1987, on a brilliantly sunny day in Pasadena, California. What a change from the gray, bitter cold of Cleveland two weeks earlier for the Broncos and their fans. Hundreds of fans from Colorado made the trip to Pasadena, for the team's first Super Sunday appearance in nine years. Super Bowl travel packages were starting to become in vogue, and Denver travel agencies had a hard time keeping up with demand for all-inclusive deals.

Although Las Vegas pegged the New York Giants as nine-and-a-half-point favorites, many pundits predicted a close game between them and the Broncos, and it was—for one half. As would be the case in their following two Super Bowls, the Broncos just fell apart at some point in the game. Up 10–9 at halftime, the Broncos suddenly had no answers for Giants quarterback Phil Simms, who would go on to have one of the greatest games in playoff history.

Simms, a smallish, blond-headed QB who looked more like singer John Denver than a football player, finished an astounding 22 of 25 passing, with 268 yards and three TD passes. His QB rating was a record 150.9. By then, Simms had established himself as a solid NFL backfield general, but nobody would have believed he'd be as good as he was that day.

"We just couldn't stop Simms in the second half," Broncos running back Steve Sewell remembers. "I thought we played pretty

BY THE NUMBERS

516—The number of times John Elway was sacked in his career—the most against any quarterback in NFL history.

well as a team that day, but they made the big plays in the end. We moved the ball pretty well on them, but we couldn't stop them in the second half."

Indeed, the Giants' vaunted defense, led by linebacker Lawrence Taylor, had a difficult time with Broncos quarterback John Elway much of the day. Elway, in his first Super Bowl appearance and fresh from his heroic "the Drive" game in Cleveland, threw for 304 yards on the day. He marched Denver right down the field on the game's first possession, before the Broncos had to settle for a 48-yard Rich Karlis field goal—which tied a Super Bowl record at the time. The Giants answered with a touchdown drive to go up 7–3, but Elway answered back with a 58-yard scoring drive late in the first quarter.

When Elway ran into the end zone from four yards out, Denver was back in the lead and New York didn't appear to have any answers for the young superstar. Denver's defense stuffed Simms on the next series, and back came Elway and the Broncos, right down the field on the ensuing possession.

On a third-and-12 play, Elway hit wide receiver Vance Johnson with a 54-yard bomb to the Giants' 28. Seven plays later, the Broncos had a first-and-goal from the 1-yard line. The Broncos would soon be up 17–7. Things were looking good.

And then everything started going bad.

The Giants' defense rose up, stuffing the Broncos on three straight plays. In fact, Denver was pushed back to the 6-yard line, after Taylor sacked Elway, and on third-and-goal, Giants linebacker Carl Banks hit Broncos back Sammy Winder in the backfield for a four-yard loss. That brought Karlis and his bare right foot back onto the field. A field goal would be a disappointment, after getting to the 1, but points were points. Besides, this would be an easy three points. Karlis was good from 48 earlier, so this would be a chip shot. Put the points on the board already.

Karlis missed the 23-yarder, wide right. It was the shortest miss in Super Bowl history. The miss stunned the Broncos and had Giants players throwing their fists in the air. But Denver's defense stayed strong, forcing another Giants punt. Elway would find a

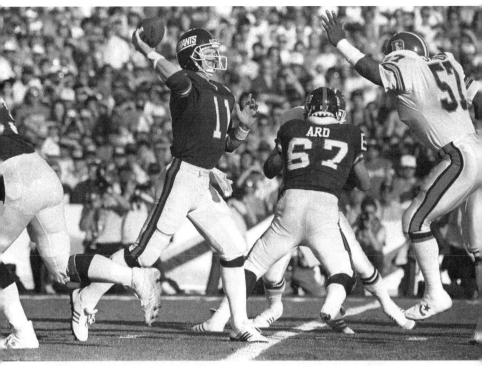

The New York Giants and quarterback Phil Simms were simply too much for leaping linebacker Tom Jackson and the Broncos in Super Bowl XXI on January 25, 1987.

way to overcome the missed opportunities of the previous drive, Denver fans believed.

But then, the Broncos got a bad break from the referees, when an Elway–to–Clarence Kay pass was ruled incomplete. Replays seemed to indicate otherwise, but the call stood and the Broncos faced third down instead of a first-and-10.

On the next play, the tide started to really swing toward the Giants. Elway went back to pass, but he was sacked in the end zone by New York defensive end George Martin. Two points for the Giants. There are few more disheartening, momentum-changing plays in football than a safety for the other guys. Not only does the other team get the two points, but they also get the ball back on the ensuing kickoff—via punt.

DEATH THREATS FROM THE HOLIDAY INN

Steve Tensi, who quarterbacked the Broncos in the late 1960s, was not beloved by the fans. The Broncos gave up two first-round draft picks to get him from San Diego, to replace Marlin Briscoe in 1969, but he never panned out. Fans vilified Tensi, booing him lustily after interceptions or incomplete passes. But at least one fan took things way too far. That fan, unidentified to this day, phoned in a death threat to the Broncos about Tensi.

The fan said he would shoot Tensi from the Holiday Inn, which was right next to Mile High and overlooked the field from its taller floors. This was the age of assassination, don't forget. Political leaders such as John F. Kennedy, Bobby Kennedy, and Martin Luther King Jr. had been gunned down in recent years, and the country was raw from violence. The Broncos—and their players—took the threat seriously. Tensi's teammates were genuinely nervous about standing near him during the game. Fortunately, nothing happened.

But again, the Broncos defense held strong. The Giants were forced to punt after the safety, and Elway got Denver to the New York 16-yard line. It was time for Karlis to atone for his earlier miss and send the Broncos into the locker room with some momentum again. Wrong. Karlis missed again, wide right. The Broncos trudged into the locker room with the lead, but they knew they'd blown some big chances to put the Giants in a sizable hole. The lead probably should have been 20–7 at the half; instead, it was just 10–9.

Giants coach Bill Parcells must have made a great halftime speech, because his team could do no wrong the rest of the way. The Giants scored a Super Bowl–record 30 points in the half, 17 in the third quarter. In that decisive third, New York outgained the Broncos in yards from scrimmage 168–2.

One of the big plays of the half was a successful fake punt by the Giants on their first possession. Backup QB Jeff Rutledge took the redirected snap and ran for a first down, bringing Simms and the offense back onto the field. Hulking Giants tight end Mark

Bavaro caught a 13-yard TD pass from Simms not long after, to start the onslaught. Phil McConkey made it 33–10 with a deflected scoring catch to start the fourth quarter, and the Giants' defense started to put more pressure on Elway.

All the great feelings from Cleveland were gone now. But 1986–87 will still be fondly remembered in Broncos history. It was the season in which Elway started to become a legend—although it would take more than another decade before he would become a champion.

FROM 10–0 TO "ARE YOU KIDDING ME?"

When Rich Karlis kicked an easy 24-yard field goal with 5:51 left in the first quarter of Super Bowl XXII, there was no doubt this time. The Broncos were going to be world champions. They had rolled over Houston and Cleveland to get to Jack Murphy Stadium in San Diego, while the NFC Redskins had struggled in their first two playoff games, against Chicago and Minnesota.

Redskins quarterback Doug Williams, a veteran who started his career with Tampa Bay in the 1970s, did not look all that great in the earlier playoff wins. Washington had a solid 11–4 regular season, but the Broncos looked like the better team now. They were the ones who had been to the Super Bowl the year before. They had learned how to win it this time. This, the third time to the Big One, would be the charm.

Not by a long shot.

In what remains a Super Bowl record, the Redskins scored 35 points in one quarter—the second—on their way to a 42–10 victory on January 31, 1988. To this day, many Broncos still can't believe it happened. "We really thought we were going to win the game, no question about it," said Karlis. "We had a 10–0 lead after

TOP FIVE

Most Yards Rushing for Opponents, Regular Season

1. 2,538—1988
2. 2,145—1960
3. 2,117—1980
4. 2,076—1967
5. 2,064—1964

the first quarter. We scored on our first play of the game. Everything seemed to be going our way finally."

Indeed, the Broncos easily stuffed Williams and the Redskins on their first series. On his first "hut" from scrimmage, Broncos QB John Elway hit receiver Ricky Nattiel with a 56-yard bomb, into the end zone. The Redskins could do nothing on the next possession, and Denver drove right back down the field.

Despite the drive stalling at the Washington 7, Karlis added three more points. On the sidelines the Redskins already looked down. Elway had an excellent regular season and guided the Broncos to 72 points in the first two playoff games. He couldn't be stopped.

And then, on Washington's first play of the second quarter, it all fell apart for Denver. Redskins receiver Ricky Sanders slipped past the Denver secondary and caught an 80-yard TD pass from Williams. Washington got the ball back and scored five plays later, on a 27-yard Williams pass to Gary Clark.

No problem, Broncos players thought. They'd take the lead again. They'd still get the job done. As incredible as it seemed at the time, Clark's TD catch would be all Washington would need. Karlis missed a 43-yard field goal on Denver's ensuing possession, and two plays later—*two plays*—Redskins running back Timmy Smith busted loose for a 58-yard scoring run. To compound matters for Broncos fans, they learned that Smith was a Denver native, a Broncos fan growing up. Now, he was breaking their hearts—again.

It was 21–10 and the quarter just got worse. Denver punted the ball away, and—bam!—Williams found Sanders again for a

BY THE NUMBERS

39-97-4—The Broncos' record was the worst of any of the eight original American Football League teams from 1960–1970. But they were the first AFL team to ever beat an NFL team—although it came in a preseason game. On August 5, 1967, Denver beat the Detroit Lions, 13–7.

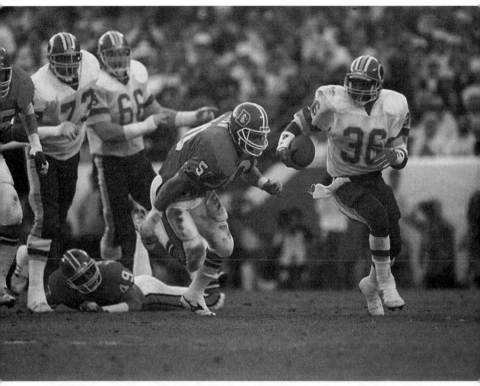

Redskins running back Timmy Smith and company ran over the Broncos defense in Super Bowl XXII on January 31, 1988.

50-yard TD pass. Another failed Broncos possession, and—boom!—Williams hit Clint Didier for an eight-yard TD toss. In a span of about 25 actual minutes, the Broncos had gone from realistic thoughts of a Super Bowl ring to no shot—none—the rest of the game.

"That was a truly bad place to be, our locker room at half-time," Karlis said. "Nobody could understand what happened. It happened so fast. You looked at the scoreboard—35–10—and it just didn't seem possible. We just couldn't get ourselves back in the game mentally from there."

The second half was one long, depressing chore for Denver fans to watch. Many didn't, turning off the game at the half. Elway could get his team only as far as the Washington 37 in the

WATCH OUT, LITTLE GIRL

In the first ever Broncos home game, October 2, 1960, at Bears Stadium, the fledgling team nearly suffered a public-relations disaster. Mary Jean McCaslin, a 13-year-old girl from the Denver suburb of Aurora, worked that first game as a member of the "Bronc-ettes" cheerleading squad. She also was the only person working the game, on the field or off, who needed to be carried off the field on a stretcher. She was bowled over by a Bronco and a Raider, after the two ran out of bounds on a play. She appeared seriously hurt at first, with several paramedics working at the scene, but it turned out she suffered nothing more than a sore neck.

Also in that game, a fan named Tom Crawford caught the football that scored the first three points in home history for the Broncos. Crawford caught Gene Mingo's kick after it split the uprights. It wasn't long, however, before a well-dressed gentleman approached Crawford and asked for the ball. It was Broncos general manager Dean Griffing, who gave no explanation for needing the ball. Crawford dutifully handed it to Griffing, who was booed by the fans on his way back to the field. It turned out that Griffing wanted the ball so it could be autographed by him and some team members, then returned to Crawford.

half. The Redskins got only seven points in the half themselves, but they certainly didn't need them.

Elway, frankly, was terrible after the first quarter. He finished just 14 for 38, with three interceptions. Denver's defense was blasted for 602 total yards of Redskins offense. Williams, a castoff supposedly washed up entering the season, would finish as the game's MVP, going 18 for 29 in the air, with 340 yards and four TDs.

"Skinned Alive" read the headline of one Denver newspaper. Local boy Smith finished with 204 yards rushing on just 22 carries—nearly 10 yards a carry on average! Denver, in the midst of a hard-hitting economic slump at the time, seemed to sag even more.

As would happen after another lopsided Super Bowl loss two years later, the Broncos reeled in the following regular season. The

1988 Broncos finished 8–8—tied for their worst full-season record since 1975. The horrible feeling of the second quarter against the Redskins just never seemed to lift that year, with the season beginning with a 21–14 loss to Seattle at Mile High Stadium.

The Broncos' leading rusher in '88 was former Dallas Cowboys star Tony Dorsett. Many hoped he could turn back the clock to his old form, but he was too far at the end of the line by then—even though he did lead Denver with 703 yards on the ground. But it always looked strange to see Dorsett in an orange uniform—much as it did to see Johnny Unitas in a Chargers uniform at the end of his career or Joe Namath in a Los Angeles Rams getup.

Elway threw for more interceptions (19) than touchdowns (17) and had just a 71.3 QB rating. The defense allowed a whopping 158.6 rushing yards per game on average—27th in the league. The low point of the season was a 42–0 loss to the Saints in New Orleans in week 12, not to mention two close losses to the Raiders.

Many Broncos fans, of course, began calling for the head of coach Dan Reeves. But owner Pat Bowlen stuck with him, and the Broncos made a fourth Super Bowl appearance the following season, against San Francisco. It didn't seem possible, but that game would prove worse than the humiliation to the Redskins.

BRIAN GRIESE: HOW DO YOU TOP THAT ACT?

Quick, name the Denver Broncos quarterback who has the highest single-season passing percentage (66.7) in team history? Who holds the team record for most consecutive games with a touchdown pass (23)? If you answered Brian Griese, go to the head of the class.

Mention Griese's name to longtime Broncos fans, however, and all you get is a sad shake of the head. "What a waste of potential" is one of the things they'll most often say.

Brian Griese was a player who had the enormous burden of not only being the son of a Hall of Fame quarterback, but also being the player who succeeded the most popular player in Broncos history and another Hall of Famer, John Elway.

By most people's estimates, Griese's career would have been considered pretty decent. But next to the careers of his father, Bob, and Elway, Griese's didn't measure up. That isn't fair, of course, but who said anything in pro football is fair?

"It was a pressure cooker, and the person that was in front of the microphone back then was a very defensive person, and probably for good reason," Griese told the *Rocky Mountain News* in 2007. "But that's not who I am. And I really feel, whether it was

Brian Griese performed admirably following in the footsteps of a legend, but was constantly running from the long shadow cast by John Elway.

OF ALL THE DAYS...

One of the real disappointments for Broncos fans during their team's first Super Bowl—besides losing to the Dallas Cowboys—was being denied the privilege of listening to the longtime radio voice of the team, Bob Martin.

The day of the game, Martin, who had been battling bone cancer for two years, began suffering intense pain in his back and legs. He had to be taken to a New Orleans hospital to undergo surgery, missing the chance to call the game.

Martin, who began calling Broncos games in 1964, had never missed a game to that point. Martin's partner in the booth, Larry Zimmer, called the play-by-play. Martin recovered, however, and continued to call games for the Broncos for another decade. He died in 1990, but is still known as "the voice of the Broncos."

right or wrong, that I got a bad rap.... I think I was a product of the situation. And I think if you put anybody in that situation, with the constant barrage of negativity, you're going to put up a wall. And then people say, 'Why aren't you as open as you should be?' Well, because every time I'm open, I feel like people are stinging me."

Indeed, Griese gained a reputation in the Denver media in his years with the Broncos (1998–2002) as being aloof or arrogant. He didn't smile much, for starters. He often gave clipped, irritated-sounding answers to questions. He didn't show a lot of emotion on the field, his expression often the same: blank.

Griese didn't help his cause in Denver with some bizarre off-field incidents. In 2002, police were called to the home of running back Terrell Davis after Griese was found unconscious in his driveway. Griese said he was running in the driveway when he tripped, fell, and hit his head. Griese said alcohol played no part, but the year before he was placed on 12 months' probation after pleading no contest to driving while impaired after failing a breathalyzer test. Another time, he sprained an ankle after he said he tripped over his dog at home.

KAY NOT ALWAYS SPECIAL

Clarence Kay played tight end for the Broncos from 1984 to 1992, making some good headlines in those years for his play. Truth be told, however, Kay's name appeared in more bad headlines during, and especially after, his career. A 6'3", 237-pound end that played collegiate football at Georgia, Kay was arrested an astonishing 12 times from 1984 to 2000. Most of his initial arrests were for substance abuse, including cocaine.

After his career ended, however, Kay was apprehended several times on charges of domestic violence and stalking. Included among the incidents was a charge that he slammed his girlfriend's head into a carport beam in April 2006, in Edgewater, Colorado. In half of Kay's first 12 arrests, the charges were dismissed, and some in the Denver community believed he got special treatment for being a Bronco.

Even after his 2006 arrest and guilty plea of harassment in a domestic violence case, Kay was sentenced to a relatively light six months in jail. Kay's constant brushes with the law were an embarrassment to the Broncos, but not enough to get rid of him in his prime. He was a good blocking tight end and coach Dan Reeves used him a lot in running schemes. Kay caught 193 passes in 135 games for Denver, with 13 touchdowns.

The Denver media had a field day, making fun of Griese, always with the added barb that he was "no John Elway." Griese responded by withdrawing from the public, giving only the most perfunctory of interviews and only meeting with the media on occasion because he had to.

Still, it wasn't all a downer for Griese in Denver. He had some good moments, including a fine 2000 season in which he completed 64.3 percent of his passes and threw for 19 touchdowns and only four interceptions. He led Denver to an 11–5 record and a playoff berth, but he had the misfortune of going up against one of the all-time great NFL defenses in the first round, the eventual Super Bowl champion Baltimore Ravens.

But that 2000 season seemed to justify coach Mike Shanahan's belief that the Broncos had a potential superstar on their hands, and why he and owner Pat Bowlen gave Griese a six-year, $39 million contract that included a record $12.6 million signing bonus.

Things started to slip, however, in 2001. Griese's completion rate (61 percent) that year was good, but he threw too many costly interceptions among his 19 overall. When Ed McCaffrey was lost to a season-ending broken left leg on opening night, Griese lost one of his favorite receivers and started looking almost exclusively downfield to Rod Smith. Opposing defenses spotted the trend quickly and picked him off a lot. Still, he did throw for 23 touchdowns in 15 starts. But the Broncos finished just 8–8, and the fingers started pointing heavily at Griese.

Shanahan gave Griese another chance in 2002, naming him starter again. He responded with the team-record 66.7 completion percentage and led Denver to a 3–0 start, 6–2 by the midway mark. But things went poorly after that.

Griese suffered a torn knee ligament in a 31–9 victory over Seattle in week 10 that got Denver to 7–3. Backup Steve Beuerlein replaced him the next two games, both overtime losses. Griese was ineffective in his return against the New York Jets, and suddenly the Broncos had just a 7–6 record. He managed a win over a mediocre Kansas City team the next week, but he would start his final game in a Broncos uniform the next, horrible week, in Oakland.

TOP FIVE

Longest Interception Return by Opponents in Broncos History

1. 103—Vencie Glenn, at San Diego, November 29, 1987
2. 99—Stanley Richard, vs. San Diego, September 9, 1994
3. 98—Rod Woodson, vs. Oakland, November 11, 2002
4. 97—Julius Peppers, vs. Carolina, October 10, 2004
5. 94—Eric Turner, at Oakland, September 20, 1998
6. 87—Ron Hall, vs. Boston, September 18, 1966
7. 86—Greg Townsend, at L.A. Raiders, December 4, 1988

In what Griese said beforehand was be the "biggest game of my pro career," he played one of his worst. He went three for eight in the first quarter, for 13 yards and two interceptions. The Raiders raced to a 21–0 lead and Griese was out of the game by the second quarter, in favor of Steve Beuerlein.

With injury added to insult, Griese also reinjured his knee after a big hit from former Broncos linebacker Bill Romanowski.

TRIVIA

What is the biggest second-half lead the Broncos have ever blown to lose a game?

Find the answers on pages 175–176.

Beuerlein rallied the Broncos in the second half, which prompted Romanowski to say he made a "mistake" by forcing Griese's exit and making the Broncos go with "a better quarterback."

The Denver media wasn't any kinder to Griese.

"The Broncos keep waiting for him to become the guiding force, but they're as misguided as his passes," wrote *The Denver Post*'s Woody Paige. "He was three of eight for 13 whole yards and the two interceptions in the opening quarter and left with a QB rating of 0.7 above his uniform number and 14.7 above a dead man's rating. How long, Mike Shanahan, how long? Four More Years? NO. Four More Games? NO. Four More Quarters? NO. Four More Downs? NO WAY! If Shanahan continues to hitch his wagon to Griese, then that horse and cart should be ridden out of Denver together."

Shanahan was never a coach to bow to media pressure, but he had seen enough of Griese by then. He would be sent packing in the off-season, with Shanahan setting his sights on free agent Jake Plummer to succeed Griese.

Griese later played for Miami—trying to revive Dolphins fans' memories of the days when his father was winning Super Bowls—but that, too, ended badly. It seemed that no matter where he went as a pro, Griese never could escape the burdens of comparison to a legend.

THE UGLY

AVERT YOUR EYES, THE BRONCOS ARE COMING

In 2006, ESPN came out with a list of the 10 ugliest uniforms in professional sports history. The Denver Broncos' first uniforms, worn in 1960 and '61, came in at number three.

Just think, in all of pro sports, in all of the various incarnations of uniforms worn by every pro team in the history of sports, only two other getups were judged uglier than the Broncos' initial togs.

How ugly were they, as the late Johnny Carson might have asked?

"They were so ugly, you literally would not want to look at yourself in the mirror," said the team's first quarterback, Frank Tripucka. "You could see people laughing at you. You'd see women putting their hands to their face and trying not to laugh. You couldn't wait to get to the locker room to take the damn things off. It was bad. I've always said you play like you look, and we looked like we had bad pajamas on or something."

The Broncos' first uniforms were not new at all. They were not even meant to be worn by professional football players. They were actually the old uniforms worn by college All-Star players, in a game called the Copper Bowl in Tucson.

That's how poor the Broncos' first ownership group was, led by Bob Howsam, who later went on to a successful career as a baseball executive in St. Louis and Cincinnati. The Broncos were so hastily assembled into the fledgling American Football League

THE TERRY BRADSHAW–JOHN ELWAY FEUD

Once upon a time, before John Elway became a two-time Super Bowl champion who went out on top, he was belittled. That it happened mainly from the media and some fans is understandable. Pro sports is one of highs and lows, slings and arrows, and even the best get skewered now and then by the peanut gallery.

But in the NFL, it has always been highly unusual for players of the same peer group to criticize one another publicly. Anyone who makes it to the NFL level earns a measure of respect that only those who played the game with them can understand.

That's why it was so shocking when, shortly after Elway was drafted by the Baltimore Colts but didn't want to play there, he was the subject of a fairly vicious verbal attack by four-time Super Bowl champion QB Terry Bradshaw.

Elway didn't want to play in Baltimore, partly because of the Colts' militaristic coach, Frank Kush. As a California boy, he wanted to play football in the West, mostly to be closer to his family. He contemplated giving up football entirely to concentrate on a Major League Baseball career, after being drafted by the New York Yankees. He even played some minor league baseball in the Yankees farm system.

Bradshaw did not like Elway's thought process, believing it a huge slight to the Colts and the NFL in general. He was quoted thusly in a national publication:

> By him saying, "'I don't want to do that' is a slap in the face for the draft and the National Football League. I could have come out of Louisiana when I was the first player picked saying, 'I don't want to go up to Pittsburgh, it's ugly, it's cold, the people don't understand a southern boy, and I want to be close to my mamma.' I could have done the same thing, but I didn't. I went, and why I went was because they were 1–13 and I said I'm going to go up there and make them a winner, and we did…. For a guy like Elway to say, 'I want to be on the West Coast, I want to be on the beach, I'm a California boy.' Well, who cares what you are? Then he says, 'I'll

play baseball.' Play baseball. He should play baseball, because in my opinion he's not the kind of guy you win championships with. He never did it when he was at Stanford and I don't think he will do it in Denver. Personally, I don't care if he never does it.

Elway was greatly upset by the comments but resisted firing back. By 1998, Bradshaw was a color analyst with Fox, which broadcast the Super Bowl that year in San Diego between Denver and Green Bay. The Denver media made a huge deal out of Bradshaw's old quote, rerunning it several times in the buildup to the game and seeking him out for further comment.

By then, however, Bradshaw was contrite. He apologized to Elway prior to his going on to win his first championship ring. But perhaps one of Elway's favorite photos has to be the one of him holding up the Vince Lombardi Trophy for the first time—with Bradshaw standing right next to him, holding a microphone and hoping for a few words from the man known previously as "not the kind of guy you win championships with."

in 1960 that management had no idea where to find players, much less things like uniforms and a place to play and practice.

After settling such details as getting a stadium, a coach, and all the other big-ticket items, new Broncos general manager Dean Griffing not only made a deal to get the hand-me-down college bowl game uniforms, but also made a deal with a Denver sporting-goods store for some "matching" socks. It has never been confirmed, but most people believe the socks came from a high school football team that didn't want them anymore.

The jerseys were described as "gold" but looked more like a sickly yellow. The pants were UPS brown, along with the helmets that featured no image of a Bronco, just plain white numerals. What really put the uniforms into a whole new level of unsightliness were the matching gold belts and the hideous vertically striped, brown-and-white socks.

"The socks were just awful," Tripucka said. "They looked like they should be worn by Bozo the Clown. No, even he wouldn't have worn them. But I guess that's the best the ownership could afford then. We knew they didn't have a lot of money."

The team was so poor that it couldn't even afford two sets of uniforms, for home and road games. Every Sunday, the Broncos, no matter the venue, trotted onto the football field looking like experiments gone horribly awry from the mind of a demented, color-blind fashion designer.

The Broncos' combined 7–20–1 record their first two seasons in the AFL, along with the awful uniforms, only cemented their image to the public as a bumbling, laughable franchise. Tripucka still enjoys looking at film of the Broncos' first years, however. But the sight of the uniforms makes him cringe.

"They were also too small," he said. "On top of how bad they looked, they were made for smaller guys. I had to cut the armpits just to be able to raise my arms."

When Griffing was relieved of his duties as Broncos GM following the team's second season, one of the first things his successor, Jack Faulkner, did was order new uniforms. Out went the brown and "gold" and in came the orange and blue that would come to symbolize the franchise to this day.

Tripucka was still around for the third season, and he was overjoyed. So were the rest of the players and fans, and to give the old uniforms a proper sendoff, a bonfire was organized prior to a July intrasquad game in Denver. Bonfires before football games are a tradition in many cities, particularly in the college ranks. Pictures or stuffed uniforms of the opposition are usually set to blaze as a rallying cry.

On that warm night in the summer of 1962, it was not the opposition, but the Broncos' uniforms, that were torched. Players and fans alike cheered as the monstrosities became flickering ashes, ascending to the place where bad uniforms go to die. There, they joined those of the Chicago White Sox and San Diego Padres, circa 1970s, Vancouver Canucks of the 1980s, and Cleveland Cavaliers of the early '80s.

Today, the socks or any other part of the Broncos' original uniforms are actually a hot commodity among collectors. They are almost impossible to find, although former Broncos head coach Red Miller—an assistant in the team's first years—said he saved a pair of socks from the bonfire and still has them.

DID YOU KNOW...

That a Broncos player named Dwight Harrison once pulled a gun on his teammates?

It's true, and, fortunately, it did not result in what could have been one of sports' biggest horror stories. In the 1972 season, Harrison, a receiver, got into a fight with fiery Broncos lineman Lyle Alzado. Harrison lost the fight and was humiliated to the point where he returned to the team's locker room later in the day, brandishing a pistol. Players hit the floor, as Harrison demanded to know Alzado's whereabouts.

"We kissed the cement so fast, it had to be a world record," said Broncos kicker Jim Turner. "All he said was, 'Where's Lyle?'"

Running back Floyd Little calmed Harrison down enough to coax him into coach John Ralston's office. Harrison, who broke down in tears, was traded later that day to the Buffalo Bills, for future star Haven Moses.

In a twisted, ironic way, Harrison did Denver a huge favor with his near-tragic loss of temper.

"May they not rest in peace," Tripucka said with a laugh. "Oh, I suppose I have a little bit of a fondness for them, I guess. It was like the saying, 'A face only a mother could love.' Well, we were their mothers I suppose. We won our first two games in those things. Maybe we won because the other team just couldn't stand the sight of us. Maybe we scared 'em to death!"

55-10: A NATIONAL EMBARRASSMENT

John Elway lost two Super Bowls prior to January 28, 1990. By big scores, too. The one title-game loss of his first three sure to elicit a scowl on Elway's famous face, however, is Super Bowl XXIV against the San Francisco 49ers. It would finish as the biggest blowout in the game's history. Nobody ever thought a team could destroy another as badly as Chicago did New England in a 46–10 Super Bowl win a few years before, but it happened at the Louisiana Superdome that day—the fourth straight time the

WATSON'S SLIP OF THE TONGUE

After retiring from the Broncos in 1987, wide receiver Steve Watson went on to work in the Denver media as a popular television personality.

In the early 1990s, however, Watson lost his job as a Broncos analyst and talk-show host with KUSA, Channel 9, after seemingly bringing his political beliefs into the open on the air. Just prior to the Denver gubernatorial election, Watson said during a broadcast of "Broncos Huddle", "I just want to wish my friend Roy Romer good luck in the election."

Watson apologized for what he said was just an innocent remark, but the station fired him anyway.

losing team finished with 10 points in Super Bowl games at the Superdome.

The halftime act was, appropriately enough, a "Peanuts" tribute. By game's end, Elway was known as the Charlie Brown of pro sports—the guy who always had the football pulled back before he ran up to kick it.

The game was impossibly one-sided. San Francisco became the first team in Super Bowl history to score two touchdowns in each quarter. The 49ers, led by Hall of Famer Joe Montana, piled up 461 yards of total offense. Denver had 167. The 49ers had the ball for 39:31, to Denver's 20:21. Montana completed 22 of 29 passes, with *five* touchdowns. Wide receiver Jerry Rice caught a record three TD passes. Elway went 10 for 26 for 108 lousy yards and two interceptions.

The Broncos joined Minnesota as the only other NFL team to be 0–4 in Super Bowls (they would soon be joined by the Buffalo Bills).

"In the aftermath of a nightmare somehow far worse than their other three, the Broncos have accomplished a first: making mediocrity more desirable than being the league runner-up," columnist Jay Mariotti wrote in *The Denver Post.* "Wouldn't they have been better off going 8–8 again than playing the role of the big easy in the Big Easy? Didn't you feel better when they were .500 last season than you do this morning?"

Fellow *Post* columnist Woody Paige was no less kind to the blue and orange. "Elvis is still not alive, and neither were the Denver Broncos yesterday," Paige wrote. "The San Francisco 49ers, as active as cats on a hot tin roof, humiliated the Broncos.... In comparison, the Falklands War was closer. The troops at the Alamo held out longer. Voltaire accurately described this game hundreds of years ago: 'They squeezed the orange and threw away the skins.'"

The game started a deterioration process in the relationship between Elway and coach Dan Reeves. For years, Elway had wanted to open up the offense more, in the mold of the 49ers. Former San Francisco coach Bill Walsh had been credited for revolutionizing pro football with his intricate "West Coast Offense." He was replaced in 1989 by rookie coach George Seifert, but the 49ers' game plan changed little.

Reeves was more of a traditional, ground-game coach. He had probably the NFL's most athletic quarterback, with the strongest arm, in Elway. But he rarely wanted to throw the ball on anything other than third down, while Montana seemed to be able to throw anytime he wanted. The Broncos felt better about running the football, however, than they had in a while entering their fourth Super Bowl. The addition of rookie running back Bobby Humphrey, who finished with 1,151 yards in the regular season, gave Reeves the confidence he could run the ball on San Francisco and slow the game down a little.

For a while, the strategy seemed sound. As they had in Elway's other two Super Bowl appearances, the Broncos started out okay. They fell behind 7–0 but responded with a 49-yard scoring drive, with David Treadwell kicking a 42-yard field goal.

Then, for one of the few times all day, the Broncos defense forced a three-and-out series. Vance Johnson returned the punt to the Broncos' 49, and Denver was in business.

And just like that, they were out of business. Humphrey fumbled the ball after being hit by 49ers lineman Kevin Fagan.

San Francisco 49ers wide receiver Jerry Rice shakes off Denver defender Dennis Smith during the 49ers' 55–10 shellacking of the Broncos in Super Bowl XXIV on January 29, 1990.

Ten plays later, Montana hit Brent Jones with a seven-yard scoring pass and it was 13–3; the kick failed. That was about the only thing that failed for San Francisco from therein.

The score was a humiliating 41–3 by the third quarter. There was no doubt by now the Broncos would become the second team in league history to lose four Super Bowls, and the jokes at Denver's expense began. "Bronco" was another word for "choke," one crack went. Denver's only TD drive of the day was capped off by Elway's three-yard run, cutting the lead to 41–10 late in the third. But the 49ers had no mercy on this day, scoring two more times. The Broncos had eclipsed the Patriots' previous record for Super Bowl futility in one game, by nine points. Elway stood on the sideline, with the lowliest look of his career. He would call the day an "embarrassment" and privately stewed that Reeves's system was antiquated in the new NFL.

But probably no game plan would have mattered against that 49ers team. Montana was in peak form, although it would be the final Super Bowl win of his career. Rice is probably the greatest wide receiver in NFL history. Running back Roger Craig was as dangerous catching passes out of the backfield as he was carrying the ball. The defense, with nasty, hard-hitting veterans such as Bill Romanowski, Matt Millen, and Ronnie Lott, was better than people credited.

The loss sent the team—and the city—into a downward spiral. Most Broncos fans were truly embarrassed at their team. After the first three Super Bowl losses, the city still threw the Broncos a parade. Not this time.

Radio talk shows lit into Reeves and Elway. Reeves was too conservative, they said, and Elway choked in the big ones. The defense didn't know how to play against more intricate NFC defenses—always playing tough against the AFC but like patsies in the big one against the other conference.

"It was doomsday under the dome. By the middle of the third quarter, it was difficult to find anyone who would admit they were from Denver," Paige wrote. No, Coloradans still had pride in their team. But nationally they were now bona fide losers. The Broncos had lost their last two Super Bowls by a combined 97–20 score. Elway seemed to be in a funk for the following 12 months. He had, for him, a mediocre 1990 regular season, throwing 15 TDs and 14 interceptions. The Broncos finished 5–11—the worst season of Elways's career. The 1990 Broncos defense was atrocious, however, allowing 30 or more points five times—including 40 to a 6–10 Detroit team. The Broncos couldn't win in the clutch, either, losing seven games by five points or less.

Most experts thought Reeves would be fired following the 5–11 season, but he lasted another two years—rebounding to 12–4 in 1991. But by 1992, things had become toxic between Elway and Reeves. After the strong '91 season, Elway was shocked and disturbed to see Reeves draft a quarterback, Tommy Maddox, in the first round of the 1992 draft. Elway was only eight years into his career, but already it seemed as if Reeves were planning for a future without him. Elway was furious, but he bit his tongue—keeping the interests of the team ahead of his.

But the slight from Reeves affected Elway's play in 1992. He threw only 10 TDs, with 17 interceptions, with just a 65.7 QB rating. Part of the problem was a shoulder injury that sidelined him for four games. The Broncos had a lousy running game, with Gaston Green leading the team with only 648 yards. The team finished 8–8, and Reeves finally was relieved of his duties by owner Pat Bowlen.

THROWBACK DAY, 1994: THROW IT BACK

As we've noted earlier in this tome, the Broncos' early uniforms never registered too highly in the fashion department. The team's first getups featured brown pants, white belts, and hideous socks that one would see on, well, circus clowns.

Their second set of uniforms wasn't much better. In place of the brown-and-white color scheme came the familiar orange, blue, and white colors that remain today. However, starting in 1962, a new logo came with the uniforms, a pudgy football player with a comically large nose being thrown into the air by a bucking bronco. The shoulder pads featured large stripes and the socks still had vertical stripes to them. Most players chose to wear the pants low enough for them not to be seen. On September 18, 1994, the Broncos, in coordination with the NFL, decided to have a "throwback jersey" day at Mile High Stadium, in a game against the hated Los Angeles Raiders. Denver came into the game with an 0–2 record, with the defense having surrendered 62 points. By the end of the day, the Broncos' defense would surrender 48 more points and suffer the worst defeat at home since a 43–7 beating by the Raiders in 1968.

Many, including some grumbling players, seemed to place some of the blame for the 48–16 drubbing on the ugly, 1965 duplicate uniforms. Quarterback John Elway, who completed just 14 of 33 passes and was replaced in the fourth quarter for one of the few times in his career, by Hugh Millen, told reporters afterward he "never want[ed] to see those uniforms again."

MORTON'S SUPER WOES

Craig Morton is well remembered by most Broncos fans for taking the team to its first Super Bowl, in 1978. But that Super Bowl, and the other one he played in during his long NFL career, didn't go so well for him. Not only did he throw four interceptions for Denver against Dallas in New Orleans, but he also threw three for the Cowboys in their 16–13 loss to the Baltimore Colts in Super Bowl V.

Wade Phillips, in his second season as head coach of the Broncos, endured heavy booing and more than a couple of obscenities from the remaining crowd as he trudged off the field. It was one thing for Broncos fans to take a big loss at home; it was another thing altogether to take it from the "Raidahs," who amassed 424 yards of total offense and laughed on their way to the team buses. It was at this point that some in the Denver media, as well as some among the fans, wondered if Elway was all washed up.

"There's gray at John Elway's temples and resignation in his eyes," wrote *Denver Post* columnist Mark Kiszla. "In the worst day anybody can remember at Mile High Stadium, it made you angry to read the scoreboard: Raiders 48, Broncos 16. It made you ashamed to hear drunks in the South Stands yell curses at owner Pat Bowlen. It made you sorry that coach Wade Phillips admitted, 'This is a low point of my life.' But the saddest sight was watching Elway limp painfully toward his locker almost an hour after the loss. For the first time in his 12-year NFL career, Elway looked old. For the first time in his 160 starts for the Broncos, it seemed very possible Elway someday will retire from football without a Super Bowl ring."

Time would prove the doubters wrong, but on that ugly September day it did seem laughable that Elway would get back to a Super Bowl anytime soon. The Broncos' defense was awful, and Elway was starting to become prone to interceptions again, like

DALE CARTER—BUSTED

In the summer of 1999, the two-time defending Super Bowl champion Broncos signed free-agent cornerback Dale Carter away from the rival Kansas City Chiefs, to a four-year, $22 million contract. The rich had just gotten richer.

Carter was a four-time Pro Bowl player who was considered the best at his position in the NFL. Even with the retirement of John Elway, many picked the Broncos to win it all again, partly because of Carter's addition.

It didn't exactly turn out that way. The '99 season was a disaster. The Broncos started 0–4, including a 26–10 loss to Carter's former team in week two.

Carter turned out to be a free-agent bust. He intercepted only two passes and the Broncos allowed 318 points—their most since 1995. Then, in the off-season following a 6–10 regular season, Carter failed an NFL drug test. He was suspended for the entire 2000 season and never played for the Broncos again. He also had to forfeit much of his signing bonus with Denver.

To his credit, Carter seemed to overcome his drug problem and played for several more years in the NFL, with Minnesota, New Orleans, and Baltimore.

early in his career. Against the Raiders, he had an interception returned for a touchdown for the third game in a row. As Kiszla noted, the futility of the 0–3 start, on top of his national reputation for not being able to win the big ones, was starting to wear on his 34-year-old face.

"This is as bad as it gets," Elway said.

Wrote Kiszla, known for his poison pen, "Elway's contract runs through 1996; his time is running short. Bowlen waited too long to build a team around him. It has been five seasons since Elway took the Broncos to the Super Bowl. Where has the time gone? Just as Elway is destined for the Hall of Fame, he's also doomed to be as decidedly average as yesterday's 151-yard performance with increasing frequency in coming years. A quarterback who relies on his arm doesn't get better with age. It's clear Elway can no longer win a championship by himself." The Broncos would not win a championship in 1994, suffering their first losing season (7–9) since 1990. But Elway, as competitive a player who ever lived and stung by the criticism, rebounded to prove he wasn't washed up yet. He actually finished the season with a 62.1 completion percentage, the second highest of his career to that point. And he led the Broncos to seven victories in the following 10 games after the Raiders debacle.

Denver actually stood with a 7–6 record entering the final three weeks, with hopes of a playoff spot still alive. But the Broncos lost all three, including a 42–19 thumping in San Francisco in week 15 and a 30–28 loss to a mediocre New Orleans team at home to close the season.

Phillips, a likable man whose father, Bum, was a former NFL head coach in Houston and New Orleans, never coached another game for the Broncos. He was fired, with one year left on his contract, by Bowlen. Phillips said he expected Bowlen to honor the last year of his deal, but it didn't happen. Some bad blood resulted, and Bowlen took some heavy criticism of his own for letting Phillips twist in the wind too long before axing him.

"Bowlen simply can't be bothered," Kiszla opined. "He's busy sipping hot cocoa at a mountain chalet until further notice. The Broncos' problems still will be there whenever the owner returns. Of course, unless somebody gets busy soon, this team's problems might still be here in 2001."

But the poisonous atmosphere would slowly dissipate, starting with the hiring of the former Raiders head coach and Broncos and 49ers assistant, Mike Shanahan. He would lead the Broncos to only a modest improvement his first season (8–8 record), but by 1996 the good times were back, thanks in no small part to a sixth-round draft choice from Georgia, a humble, likable running back named Terrell Davis.

HAIL THE JAGWADS

On January 4, 1997, the Broncos played the Jacksonville Jaguars in an AFC divisional playoff game at Mile High Stadium. The

Jaguars, a recent expansion team, were given absolutely no chance to beat the 13–3 Broncos.

That was especially the opinion of the Denver media, notably famed *Denver Post* columnist Woody Paige. A descendant of legendary Confederate Civil War cavalry general Nathan Bedford Forrest, the Tennessee native Paige could boil the blood of opposing cities with his written words.

This is how Paige began his entry in the January 4, 1997, edition of the paper: "Jacksonville Jagwads? What league are they in? When did the NFL start letting USFL teams participate in the playoffs? Did I miss something? Or, are the Jags from that goofy World League or the Continental Basketball Association? After the Broncos dispense with these Jagwads today, do they face the Barcelona Bobcats or the Birmingham Power & Light?"

Broncos fans might have smugly chortled along with Paige's column. After all, the Broncos didn't lose a single game at home in the regular season and had lost only one playoff game at home in team history. Did the Jaguars really think they had any shot of winning in Denver, against John Elway, Terrell Davis, and Mike Shanahan?

"How do you get worked up to play somebody called Jacksonville with a bunch of nobodies?" Paige wrote. "They must think they belong here, but they will learn. Jacksonville reportedly has the number-one-ranked passing game in the NFL. Wait until the Jagwads try that stuff at Mile High Stadium. And the Jags bring back center Dave Widell, who was a nice player and swell talk-show host in Denver in his day. This is easy. It will not be a Jag War. The tanned, rested, and ready Broncos will invalidate the Jagwads. Instead of 'The Drive' and 'The Fumble,' Denver-Jacksonville will be known as 'The Blowout.' The Broncos are favored by 14. Not enough."

This was bulletin-board stuff for the Jags, no question. But did that sort of thing really work? Can pro athletes really get fired up over a newspaper column, written by a middle-aged man? On January 4, 1997, the answer seemed to be yes.

"[I] wanted to thank [Paige]," Jaguars coach Tom Coughlin said following Jacksonville's 30–27 victory. "He did a nice job this

REEVES VERSUS THE SOUTH STANDS

The South Stands at Mile High Stadium (and, to a much lesser extent, at Invesco Field) was a cauldron of passion—and that word encompasses everything, from sarcasm and hostility to unbridled joy. The South Stands was the place Broncos players—and coaches—knew they needed to prove themselves the most. Dan Reeves certainly knew that, in his many years of coaching the Broncos.

Reeves heard the cheers and the boos, and occasionally worse than that. One of those times came in the troubled 1990 season in which the Broncos finished 5–11. In the final game of the year, popular running back Sammy Winder was in his last moments as a Bronco—he had decided to retire.

Fans wanted Winder to get a chance at scoring a touchdown in the final minutes, but no play was called for him.

"That's chicken shit!" a fan yelled at Reeves from the South Stands, as he exited the field.

"I'll meet you any day," Reeves yelled back, having to be restrained. Reeves still hadn't calmed down by his press conference, saying his toughness was not open to question by anybody. A few years later, as coach of the Atlanta Falcons, Reeves had a heart attack. He learned not to let the criticism from fans and media get to him anymore—no doubt a good thing for his health.

morning.... I mean that was an out-and-out flagrant violation of respect. There's no call for that."

In Broncos history, the first four Super Bowl losses have to rank as the toughest losses for their fans. But the loss to Jacksonville—Jacksonville!—on that mild day in January might rank as number five. This was supposed to be the best Broncos team ever, with a powerhouse offense, mastermind head coach, and intangibles galore, such as finally getting a Super Bowl for Elway. Somebody forgot to inform southpaw Jaguars quarterback Mark Brunell, who flat out outplayed the Hall of Famer Elway.

The game started out just according to Paige's—and everybody else's—prediction. The Broncos scored on two of their first three possessions, but the day's ultimate abnormality was foreshadowed after Denver's first two touchdowns; on the first, the extra point was blocked. After the second, a two-point conversion attempt failed. Still, Denver's 12–0 lead—an ugly football score—seemed safe already, with points-after inconsequential.

Wrong.

Brunell was brilliant after that. He guided the Jaguars to scores on their next six possessions, giving Jacksonville a 23–12 lead. Davis, who had a brilliant sophomore season with 1,538 yards rushing, ran for a touchdown and also the two-point conversion to cut it to 23–20. But Brunell, on a third-and-five play from the Broncos' 16, threw his second touchdown pass of the game, this one to receiver Jimmy Smith, to make it 30–20 with 3:39 left in the game. Elway got Denver back to within three with a 15-yard TD pass to Ed McCaffrey with 1:50 left. But there was no Mile High magic in the end. Brunell milked the clock to all zeroes, and the Jaguars had their first-ever playoff victory—in a stadium that will go down as one of the toughest for visitors to win in NFL history.

Rugged, Rocky Mountain Denver seemed to collectively stagger from the loss. This could not happen. Didn't everybody read Paige's column? Elway walked off the field looking positively shell-shocked. Some fans wept in their seats. Maybe the Broncos really would *never* win a Super Bowl.

"Without a question, this is the toughest loss I've ever faced," Shanahan told reporters afterward. "You work the whole year for this opportunity to play in our home...then somebody comes in and takes the game away from us. It hurts a lot."

"I don't have any emotions right now," Denver cornerback Lionel Washington said. "I'm numb."

Years later, Broncos offensive lineman Mark Schlereth would continue to call the Jacksonville loss the "worst day of my pro career. It was just incomprehensible to us at the time that we could lose that football game. But Brunell played a tremendous game. And I think we kind of expected them to roll over after we

It was a long day in Denver as defensive end Tony Brackens and the Jacksonville Jaguars dragged down John Elway and the Broncos with an upset win in the 1997 playoffs.

got out to a quick lead. When that didn't happen, I think it kind of knocked us off stride a little and shocked us, and by the time we got ourselves back in it, it was too late."

It had to be the happiest of moments when Jacksonville fans picked up their papers on January 5. Paige's incendiary column had been widely reprinted and broadcast throughout the city the day before, and hundreds of angry emails and phone calls poured into the *Post's* sports office.

Now what did Paige have to say?

"The columnist was unavailable for comment following the game," Paige wrote, in a humble column entitled "D(isaster)-Day in Denver."

NEW YEAR'S EVE, 2006: BLACK SUNDAY

Sun peeked through the clouds for the first time in several days on Sunday, December 31, 2006, in Denver. The worst blizzard in eight years had fallen a little more than a week before, and another smaller but potent storm added several more inches of snow to the Front Range a few days later.

The city was finally starting to dig itself out, after a state of emergency had been declared by Colorado governor Bill Owens, with Denver International Airport and most other city facilities closed down for days.

As they had numerous times before, Coloradans looked to their football team for more cheering up. The Broncos were set to play the 6–9 San Francisco 49ers that day, and a win at Invesco Field at Mile High would put the team into the playoffs the next weekend, at New England—a team the Broncos had beaten already that season in Foxborough, Massachusetts, and the year before in a post-season game that dethroned the two-time Super Bowl champs.

No way the Broncos would lose; not at home, not with a playoff berth at stake, not to a bad team like the 49ers. And not with a hotshot rookie quarterback named Jay Cutler, who was just starting to emerge as a force with the Broncos.

But it happened, and as bad as Broncos fans would feel that night, they would be shocked and saddened to tears by the events of the following morning.

In the wee hours of New Year's Day, not long after the Broncos had lost 26–23 in overtime to San Francisco, defensive back Darrent Williams—a popular, second-year starter—was killed in a drive-by shooting outside a Denver nightclub.

In a span of about 12 hours, the Broncos saw their season come to a premature end and the life of one of their youngest and most talented players come to a far briefer, more tragic end.

"All of us are devastated by this tragedy," Broncos owner Pat Bowlen said, later that day. "To lose a young player, and more important, a great young man such as Darrent Williams, is incomprehensible. To lose him in such a senseless manner as this is beyond words."

Williams, age 24, was part of a group of people, including Broncos receiver Javon Walker, who piled into a Hummer limousine after a visit to a Denver nightclub called The Shelter. Nobody was in much of a celebratory mood that night, after the shocking loss to the 49ers. Williams, a lover of music, was doing some promotional work that night for a Fort Worth, Texas, rap album label he hoped to develop. The limousine had been rented days beforehand, in anticipation of a fun night.

But there was an apparent altercation involving unknown suspects and members of Williams's party outside the club. After the

Darrent Williams prepares to return a punt against the San Francisco 49ers on December 31, 2006. According to Denver police Williams was shot and killed early the next morning in a drive-by shooting in downtown Denver.

Hummer departed, another sport utility vehicle chased it and someone fired 14 bullets into the Hummer, one of which fatally struck Williams in the neck.

"Darrent the player and Darrent the man were the same person," Broncos safety Nick Ferguson told *The Denver Post*, a day later. "He had that confidence, he had that swagger, on and off the field. To have that as a second-year player, I wish I had that type of confidence early on. Darrent would do things in practice that would make practice not seem like work. He wasn't just another teammate. That's one thing about playing here, there was a special bond we had amongst ourselves."

Williams came out of Oklahoma State and had an excellent rookie season in 2005 for Denver, unseating veteran Lenny Walls for the starting right cornerback job. He had the unenviable role of being the opposite cornerback next to Pro Bowl superstar Champ Bailey. As a result, opposing quarterbacks rarely threw near Bailey, which increased the workload dramatically for Williams.

"At his position, you're going to have ups and downs, because you're going against star receivers week in and week out," Broncos running back Tatum Bell, who was supposed to go to the same nightclub that night but changed plans, told the *Post*. "But if he had a tough game, he'd bounce back. If I was down about something, he'd pick me up. Man, I'm going to miss him. I can't believe it."

The shooting rocked Denver to the core. It was the third professional athlete to be shot in the city since 2003, with Pittsburgh Steelers star Joey Porter and Julius Hodge, a member of the Denver Nuggets, also victimized. Unlike Williams, they survived.

Broncos coach Mike Shanahan had a special fondness for Williams. Partly, it was because of Williams's tenacious spirit as a person and player. Listed at 5'8", 188 pounds, Williams was considered too small to excel as an NFL regular by some pundits, especially against the NFL's bigger, modern-day receivers.

But Williams, a father of two, gave no quarter on the field. As Bell described, he always stayed positive on and off the field, no matter the score or circumstances. His enthusiasm for the game was infectious, and Shanahan believed, over time, Williams would have developed into an All-Pro. He never got the chance.

"We all know that Darrent was an excellent player, but as a person, he was a first-class young man who brightened every room with his smile, attitude, and personality," Shanahan said. "I cannot express how heartsick I feel at this loss."

Wrote *Denver Post* columnist Mark Kiszla: "Twenty-four hours before the death of Williams, the Broncos believed they were bound for the NFL playoffs. They will now be attending a funeral."

A memorial fund was set up by the team after Williams's death. The purpose of the fund was to benefit Darrent's two children for future educational and health needs. Contributions can be sent to Darrent Williams Children's Fund, c/o Denver Broncos, 13655 Broncos Parkway, Englewood, CO 80112.

THE NUMBERS DON'T LIE (OR DO THEY?)

63 YARDS—AND THEN SOME

Jason Elam was a free spirit as a player and person. The longtime place-kicker for the Broncos flew small airplanes in his spare time and had some quite hairy tales to tell from it, including the time in Alaska when he had a simultaneous emergency landing along with a near bear attack.

Flying was part of Elam's gung-ho, gambling nature. On the football field, he always loved the pressure of kicking a ball through skinny uprights from great distances. On October 25, 1998, with four seconds left in the first half of a game at Mile High Stadium against the Jacksonville Jaguars, Elam went for one of the NFL's oldest records—one many people thought would never be tied or broken.

On November 8, 1970, Tom Dempsey of the New Orleans Saints kicked a 63-yarder against the Detroit Lions. Born with a deformed right foot, Dempsey wore a special, square-toed shoe that some believe gave him an unfair advantage in kicking footballs long distances. In fact, many NFL purists refused to consider Dempsey's feat a "real" record. But to most others, Dempsey's handicap provided astonishment that he could even kick a ball, let alone one for 63 yards.

For 28 years, Dempsey's record was considered one of pro sports' most hallowed numbers. There were Hank Aaron's 755

Jason Elam booted an NFL record-tying 63-yard field goal in 1998.

home runs, Joe Dimaggio's 56-game hitting streak, Roger Bannister's four-minute mile. And Dempsey's 63-yard field goal.

As kickers became stronger and the benefits of kicking a football soccer-style became more proven, however, it seemed only a matter of time before somebody challenged Dempsey's mark. It finally happened at Mile High, when Elam took the field, with the Broncos on the Jacksonville 46-yard line and time about to expire on the half. "Can you make it?" Broncos coach Mike Shanahan asked Elam. "I think I can get it there," Elam replied.

BY THE NUMBERS

2,675—The number of season tickets sold for Denver's first season, in 1960.

73,972—The number sold in 2006.

Actually, Elam had tried to break Dempsey's record earlier in his career. On December 10, 1995, Shanahan let Elam try a 66-yarder to end the first half at home against Seattle. The kick missed, but everyone knew Elam had the leg to challenge the record. He once kicked a 72-yard field goal at a Broncos practice—but kicking a ball in practice, with no pressure from a defense and a set holder is a lot different from a game.

"Whoo! Let's go for the record," said Tom Rouen, the Broncos punter who also spotted kicks for Elam. The snapper was David Diaz-Infante, who had missed the first six games because of arthroscopic knee surgery.

Infante's snap was a bit high, but Rouen grabbed it and quickly placed the ball down, with the traditional laces pointing toward the goal posts. Elam put all his might into it.

"Right away, I knew it had a good chance," Elam recalled, years later. "I knew I'd gotten a good piece of the ball."

Like a golfer who wills on a putt, or a hitter who tries to wave a ball fair, Elam skipped down the field in the direction of the ball as it flew toward the posts. Much of the crowd was unaware that this was a shot at Dempsey's record, as there was no timeout by either team prior to the kick. It was fourth down for Denver, and many fans had made their way to the concession stands. The Broncos had just taken a delay-of-game penalty, too, which some believed intentional, that backed the ball up to the record-tying distance.

But many did know this might make history, and the crowd noise built as the ball got closer and closer. It was going to be tight, no question about it. It might have to hit the crossbar and bounce over to make it, but it still looked like it might—might—have a chance. The ball cleared the crossbar by a couple of yards, it turned out. Elam jumped up and down, throwing his fist in the air. Rouen grabbed him in celebration and was soon joined by everyone on the team. "Jason Elam has just tied the record for longest field goal in NFL history—63 yards!" read the Mile High video screen.

Broncos ballboy, Dave Wade, caught the ball as it went over the crossbar. He immediately gave it to equipment manager Doug West, who then handed it to Elam. The Broncos went on to beat Jacksonville, 37–24, their 20th straight home victory and 12th straight overall. "I thought they were crazy," Jacksonville defensive end Renaldo Wynn told reporters after the game. "I knew he had a strong leg, but I thought there was no way he was going to make it. It went such a long distance and the only thing you could do was stand back and watch it fly. It just kept going, and going...and going."

FAST FACTS

Broncos home record from 1960 to 2000, Bears Stadium/Mile High Stadium/University of Denver Stadium: 191–109–7 (.634).

The Denver Post contacted Dempsey the day Elam tied his record. Dempsey, selling cars at the time in New Orleans, told the paper, "He'll be talking about it for a long time. I've been."

Today, the ball and shoe Elam used to kick reside in the Pro Football Hall of Fame, in Canton, Ohio. Entering the 2007 season, he still shared the record with Dempsey. While a longer field goal has been kicked in college football, nobody has yet been able to kick one 64 yards in the NFL.

But Elam knows that day will likely come—and he might get a phone call like the one to Dempsey.

"Records are made to be broken," he said. "But it's been nice having my name in the record books all this time. It's something I'll never forget, obviously. It's been an honor just to play the game as long as I have."

Elam finished the 2006 season strong, and entered 2007 as the franchise's all-time scoring leader with 1,672 points, with an amazing 568 career point-after completions in 571 attempts. He also has the second-longest Super Bowl field goal in history (51 yards), with 36 field goals beyond 50 yards.

And, one beyond 60.

HEY, CANTON, WHAT ABOUT DENVER?

In 2006, if you had asked any member, past or present, of the Broncos organization what his or her number one complaint was about the team's history, it would have been no contest: the fact that only one player, John Elway, was in the Pro Football Hall of Fame in Canton, Ohio.

Yes, Tony Dorsett and Willie Brown are in the Hall and played for the Broncos. But both played only briefly in Denver and are certainly not remembered for wearing orange and blue.

The Chicago Bears, who won one fewer Super Bowl than Denver in the first 40 years of the Super Bowl and participated in four fewer championship games than Denver, had 26 players in the Hall of Fame entering 2006. The Cleveland Browns, who still haven't won a Super Bowl, had 16 in the Hall. Granted, teams

---

DID YOU KNOW...

That legendary wide receiver Jerry Rice played his last NFL football game as a Bronco?

It doesn't show up on any stat sheets, but Rice played in the preseason with Denver in 2005, trying to extend his Hall of Fame career under former San Francisco offensive coordinator Mike Shanahan.

But Rice wasn't happy with his projected role on the team, as a backup receiver, and retired before the start of the regular season. Though he didn't say it publicly, Rice was also less than thrilled receiver Rod Smith would not give up the No. 80 jersey for him. Rice wore the number throughout his career, but so did Smith, and the veteran Bronco wasn't about to change—even for the greatest receiver of all time.

Rice wore No. 19 in his brief stay with the Broncos, catching four passes for 24 yards.

---

such as Cleveland and Chicago predate the Broncos, but it's not like football is new around the Mile High City. Dwight D. Eisenhower was president when the Broncos played their first game.

And the fact remains that only one team, San Francisco, had a better record in the NFL from 1983 to 1998, and only two franchises, Pittsburgh and Dallas, have gone to as many Super Bowls as Denver's six since the game started in 1967.

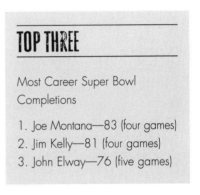

TOP THREE

Most Career Super Bowl Completions

1. Joe Montana—83 (four games)
2. Jim Kelly—81 (four games)
3. John Elway—76 (five games)

But there are the Broncos, below teams such as New Orleans, Arizona, Philadelphia, San Diego, and Seattle, on the list of franchises with numbers of players in Canton.

Every pro team has a gripe list of players they think should be in the Hall of Fame. It's part of sports. But Denver's list is long, and several probably have been unjustly kept out of the Hall, for whatever reason.

Offensively, the names at the top of the list include Jim Turner, Floyd Little, Terrell Davis, Lionel Taylor, Gary Zimmerman, Haven Moses, and Rick Upchurch. Defensively, the slights are considered even more egregious. Denver had some truly great defensive players, such as Randy Gradishar, Steve Atwater, Dennis Smith, Tom Jackson, Rich Jackson, Karl Mecklenburg, Lyle Alzado, Billy Thompson, and Louis Wright.

None of them are in the Hall of Fame. Of those names, on both sides of the ball, probably no two are mentioned more than Little and Gradishar as deserving enshrinement. Let's make the case for both, starting with Little.

When he retired in 1975, Floyd Little was the NFL's seventh all-time leading rusher, with 6,323 yards. The six running backs ahead of him (Jim Brown, O.J. Simpson, Jim Taylor, Joe Perry, Leroy Kelly, and John Henry Johnson) are all in the Hall of Fame today. Entering 2006, 39 running backs were enshrined in

TOP 10

Most Pass Attempts by an Opponent in a Game (Regular Season)

1. 62—At New York Jets, December 3, 1963
2. 60—At New Orleans, November 21, 2004
3. 59—At New England, October 8, 1995
4. 56—vs. Houston, October 17, 1965
5. 55—vs. San Diego, September 12, 1993
6. 54—vs. Kansas City, October 17, 1994
7. 54—vs. Kansas City, November 16, 1986
8. 53—vs. Washington, October 9, 2005
9. 53—vs. Oakland, November 13, 2000
10. 53—at San Diego, November 29, 1998

Canton, but Little wasn't one of them. And yet, Little still had better rushing numbers than 24 of those 39 Hall of Famers.

So why is Floyd Little not in the Pro Football Hall of Fame?

"Beats me," says former teammate Billy Thompson. "I know we didn't have very good teams in the early years of his career, but, still, look at the numbers. The fact is, he was the best running back in the NFL in his prime. And the thing is, he was and is such a class guy, such a great role model for kids. There wasn't anything he wouldn't do for kids in Denver, no cause too small that he wouldn't give his time for. Wouldn't the NFL want to remember and honor a guy like that?"

Those who say, "Hey, Floyd Little's top rushing year was 1971, 1,133 yards. Edgerrin James ran for 1,709 yards for Indianapolis in 2000, and nobody's pushing his name for the Hall," remember this: the NFL schedule in Little's day was 14 games, not 16, and running backs didn't carry the ball as much. Little got his 1,133 yards on 284 carries. James got his on 387 carries. Big difference.

Turner is one of the people, however, who doesn't believe Little is quite deserving of a place in Canton. The former kicker, who had his own radio show in Denver for years following his retirement and was known for his outspoken nature, said Little was a "very good player" and "good teammate," but the numbers don't quite add up.

"I don't think he's a Hall of Fame player," Turner said. "Otis Armstrong, on our team, was better. Matt Snell and Emerson Boozer [Turner's former teammates with the New York Jets] were better."

Still, from 1968 to 1973, nobody gained more yards rushing or from the line of scrimmage than Little. This, on some really bad teams, where he was the only guy opposing defenses thought about. He was named to the NFL's All-Pro team of the 1970s by writers, but, strangely, some of those same writers have chosen to bypass Little for induction to Canton. Little hasn't lost hope he might make it from the Hall's Seniors Committee, but the fact that he hadn't made it yet for 31 years after he retired meant the proud man from New Haven, Connecticut, wasn't holding his breath anymore.

Now let's make the case for Gradishar.

Randy Gradishar was named to the Pro Bowl seven times. This, in an era when the AFC was loaded with offensive stars that the Broncos middle linebacker had to face all the time. As a college player at Ohio State, Gradishar was called by legendary coach Woody Hayes the "best linebacker I ever coached."

Drafted 14th overall by Denver in 1974, Gradishar was an NFL Pro Bowl player by 1975. In 1978, he was named the NFL's Defensive Player of the Year.

One of the toughest players in league history, and one of its greatest tacklers, Gradishar's lack of immortality in Canton is thoroughly confusing to Broncos fans—not to mention football fans from everywhere.

"An absolutely great player," Thompson says. "Great teammate, great guy—but a great, great player.

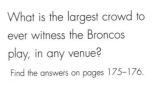

TRIVIA

What is the largest crowd to ever witness the Broncos play, in any venue?

Find the answers on pages 175–176.

He never took a play off, never went anything less than full out. I still can't believe he's not in the Hall yet."

Said Turner, simply: "It's a sin Randy's not in."

In his 10 years in the NFL, all with Denver, Gradishar led his team in tackles in all but his rookie year. He had 20 career interceptions and never missed a game in his 145-game career. He was the anchor of a defense that was ranked number one in the NFL in 1977 and 1979, and third in 1976.

In 1998, Gradishar was inducted into the College Football Hall of Fame. But nearly a decade later, he was still absent from Canton.

Nobody seems to be able to come up with a good reason why.

THE TWO JAKES

Jake Plummer is one of only three Broncos quarterbacks to take the team to an AFC championship game. He is also one of the few to lose his starting job in the middle of a season—and to a rookie, no less. Before a November 23, 2006, game in Kansas City, a report leaked out that it would be Plummer's last start of the season. He would be replaced the following game, the report said,

Jake Plummer's tenure in Denver was rocky, but he contributed greatly to the team and the community.

by first-year, former Vanderbilt QB Jay Cutler.

Despite silence from the Broncos, the report turned out to be true. Plummer would not start another game all season, seeing only brief action in week 16—the horrific New Year's Eve game against San Francisco.

It was an inglorious end in Denver for Plummer, one that, a year before, would have seemed

TOP FIVE

Highest Takeaway/Giveaway Ratio in Broncos History

1. 21—1984 (55–34)
2. 20—2005 (36–16)
3. 19—2000 (44–25)
4. 13—1964 (53–40)
5. 12—1977 (39–27)

highly unlikely. It was Plummer, after all, who led the Broncos to the 2006 AFC title game, at home against Pittsburgh. Along the way, his play helped dethrone two-time defending Super Bowl champion New England at Invesco Field.

A quarterback who liked to scramble and throw off the run—especially to his left—Plummer posted a 32–11 record as a starter in his first three years with the Broncos, after leaving the Arizona Cardinals in 2003 to sign a free-agent contract.

Plummer's No. 16 jersey became a huge seller in Colorado. He was popular with fans for his refreshing candor, although he did have a moody side that occasionally turned sour. He was involved in a "road rage" incident after a fender bender with a Denver man one time. Another time, he left an obscenity-filled voice mail to a Denver gossip columnist, Penny Parker, after she wrote about his love life. But the real, off-the-field Plummer was a man who loved doing things for others. He did countless charitable activities for the Broncos—some publicized, some not. While with the Cardinals, he created the Jake Plummer Foundation, which helped the young and old. It gave money to numerous children's causes, but also supported research to combat Alzheimer's disease.

Every year, he held a bowl-o-rama, which raised nearly $1 million for charity. He became even more civically involved following the death of former Cardinals teammate Pat Tillman—the former defensive back with Arizona who left the NFL to serve the army in Afghanistan and was killed by friendly fire.

Plummer defied an NFL edict by wearing Tillman's number for a while with the Broncos, and he occasionally spoke out against the Iraq War on behalf of the Tillman family.

TRIVIA

Who has kicked the longest punt in Broncos team history, and how long was it?

Find the answers on pages 175–176.

By the end of the 2006 season, however, Plummer was a sad sight on the Broncos sideline. He just never could get things going that year, even though Denver got off to a good start and looked a cinch to make the playoffs by midseason. The accuracy of his passing arm deserted him. In 2005, Plummer went 229 straight passes without an interception, but they became commonplace by the time coach Mike Shanahan decided to bench him in favor of the unproven Cutler.

Plummer could have created a firestorm around the team over his humiliating demotion, but the team-first, classy side of his personality won out. He kept his mouth shut, dutifully handled point-after attempts for kicker Jason Elam, and offered pats on the helmet in support of Cutler, win or lose.

"Jake is a good guy, a team guy," Elam said. "He did a lot of great things for the Broncos organization."

Plummer's best moment with the Broncos was probably the 27–13 AFC playoff win over New England on January 14, 2006, at Invesco Field. He completed 15 of 26 passes for 197 yards. He put the game out of reach with a four-yard scoring pass to Rod Smith early in the fourth quarter, outplaying the Patriots' three-time champion QB, Tom Brady.

The following week, however, things started to go bad for Plummer in Denver. He did not play very well in a 34–17 loss in the conference title game to Pittsburgh, throwing two interceptions. Plummer also fumbled the ball away twice, both times leading to Pittsburgh points. Still, the future looked good for Jake the Snake. He was the starting QB of a team that went 13–3 in 2005, and he was also becoming known as a clutch player—the game against the Steelers notwithstanding. From 1997 to 2005,

Plummer led his teams to 21 fourth-quarter comeback victories—second only to Drew Bledsoe's 24. He wasn't quite a John Elway when it came to comebacks, but Plummer inspired confidence in fans and teammates with his no-fear persona.

That's what made his end in Denver so shocking. It could have all turned around for him again, though, in the final game of 2006, against the 49ers. He was forced into the game after Cutler suffered a concussion, and fans rallied to his cause. The stage was set for Plummer to triumphantly lead the Broncos to the playoffs, which a victory over the mediocre 49ers would have done.

But it wasn't meant to be. Plummer was ineffective in relief, and Cutler later returned to the game and nearly pulled it out for Denver. Plummer was gracious in the locker room afterward, although he didn't say much to reporters. He preferred to quietly thank his teammates for all they'd done for him, and the feeling was mutual. Whatever the fans said about Plummer—and he had his detractors by the end—he was a well-respected player in the locker room.

The loss was forgotten by everyone less than 24 hours later, after Broncos defender Darrent Williams was killed in a drive-by shooting after attending a Denver nightclub.

TOP FIVE

Longest Nonscoring Passes in Broncos History

1. 88—Brian Griese to Byron Chamberlain, vs. Green Bay, October 17, 1999
2. 86—John Elway to Vance Johnson, vs. L.A. Raiders, September 26, 1988
3. 86—Craig Morton to Steve Watson, vs. Kansas City, December 6, 1981
4. 78—John Elway to Rod Smith, vs. Kansas City, August 31, 1997
5. 76—Hugh Millen to Anthony Miller, vs. San Francisco, December 17, 1994

Many times when an athlete dies tragically, players and media types like to say how it put the game "in perspective." Jake Plummer never needed that kind of shock to the system to know football was, really, an insignificant part of life. It was why he put so much time into making better the lives of those less fortunate—before he was a "star" and after.

IT AIN'T OVER 'TIL IT'S OVER

"WE GOT 'EM RIGHT WHERE WE WANT 'EM"

January 11, 1987, was a lovely day for football at Cleveland Stadium. The wind whipping off Lake Erie produced a chill factor in the negative numbers. The overcast skies had a front-row seat to the football field. Cleveland Stadium opened on July 3, 1932, and not much had changed in its cavernous environs in the intervening 55 years. The antiquated structure was nicknamed the "Mistake by the Lake," but to Clevelanders, it was home, and Judy Garland always said there's no place like home.

The Cleveland Browns of 1986–87 were a fine football team. A tough, hard-hitting defense, a hotshot quarterback out of Miami named Bernie Kosar, and a smart coach named Marty Schottenheimer had rabid Browns fans believing their team would return to the championship days not seen since Jim and Paul Brown ruled the field's patchy turf.

The Browns on this day had home-field advantage for the 1987 AFC championship game—and what an advantage it figured to be. Not only were the Browns an intimidating team, but so were their fans. Browns fans turned the lake at the end of the field into a rabid "Dawg Pound," with thousands of spectators woofing like crazed canines and pelting the field with Milk Bone brand dog biscuits.

It was here that the Broncos were given the task of winning their first playoff road game in team history and the right to go to their first Super Bowl since 1977, in what figured to be sunny Pasadena, California.

Cleveland had Brown Fever in the days leading up to the game. Dawg-woofing broke out among the well-heeled patrons the night before at stately Severance Hall, an orchestral music house. Broncos defenders Jim Ryan and Karl Mecklenburg were eating dinner at a fancy restaurant the night before when more spontaneous woofing broke out. Fans woofed and honked their horns around the Broncos' hotel all night prior to the game, doing anything they could to drive Denver players crazy.

Imagine the woofing, then, that was about to break out in another five minutes, 43 seconds. That was the amount of time left in the title game after Kosar gave Cleveland a 20–13 lead with a 48-yard touchdown bomb to receiver Brian Brennan.

Another 5:43 and it would be the Browns, not the Broncos, on their way to Pasadena to face the New York Giants. That scenario seemed a fait accompli when Browns kicker Mark Moseley's ensuing kickoff hit the dirt-patch frozen turf at the 15-yard line and bounced past Broncos return man Ken Bell. When Bell back-tracked and finally picked up the ball, a swarm of Browns tackled him just shy of the 2-yard line. All the Broncos and their young quarterback, John Elway, had to do was go 98½ yards on a frozen field against a tough defense, in front of 80,000 woofing, dog-bone-hurling Browns fans—all just to tie the game. Or else the season was over. No pressure there. It was in the Broncos huddle, before the first play was called on what would be immortalized as "The Drive," that Broncos lineman Keith Bishop uttered probably the most famous inspirational slogan in team history. "We got 'em right where we want 'em," Bishop told his cold, desperate, huddled teammates.

Many Broncos players would admit after the game they had little hope when The Drive started. Bishop's words seemed mere false bravado. "I think most guys would say things were mighty bleak at that moment," kicker Rich Karlis said. "We hadn't given up or anything, but there didn't seem a lot of hope."

From that moment on, Broncos fans would never again lose hope, as long as Elway was on the field. With 5:34 left when The

HURRY UP ON THAT FIELD!

It was a rush job for Denver public works officials in getting Bears Stadium ready for the Broncos' first home game, in 1960. In fact, the dressing rooms for the Broncos and Raiders still weren't finished by the day of the game, with patchwork plaster residue everywhere. The 25" x 90" scoreboard the team wanted to install wasn't ready, either, leaving a primitive-looking board underneath the press box to serve as the only one for fans to see. A new parking lot, at West 17th Avenue and Clay Street, was graded and covered with gravel but still hadn't been paved by game day.

Drive started, Elway orchestrated his team down the field in master fashion, culminating in a five-yard "low heater" Elway pass to Mark Jackson with 42 seconds left.

The Drive started with an important five-yard Elway pass to Sammy Winder, giving the Broncos room to operate outside of their end zone. Winder ran the ball the next three plays, getting out to the Broncos 15. From that second-and-seven play on, until the Broncos scored, Elway would either run or throw the football the next 12 plays. Most people only remember Elway's low heater to Jackson for the touchdown on The Drive, but there was an earlier, gigantic pass to Jackson that kept it going. Probably the biggest play of the entire drive was a 20-yard pass to Jackson on third-and-18 to the Browns 28-yard line. Elway had just been sacked for an eight-yard loss on second down, and the Browns and their fans sensed victory at hand. When the third-down play began, it almost ended before Elway got his hands on the ball.

Because of the crowd noise, Elway went to a silent cadence. Receiver Steve Watson was set in motion, which is when disaster nearly struck. Center Billy Bryan's snap to Elway, in the shotgun formation, was a little early. The ball grazed off Watson's left hip as he jogged past Elway in front, causing the ball to wobble down and to Elway's left. Despite the distraction of the oncoming Browns rush, Elway managed to snag the ball before it hit the ground. Had it done so, Elway no doubt would have been sacked and the Broncos would have faced about a fourth-and-30 situation. Instead, Elway stepped up in the pocket, got good protection from his line, and hit Jackson with a perfect pass to the Browns 28-yard line. It was the speedy Jackson's first reception of the day, and a big one.

Previously, the Broncos advanced 22 yards, to the Browns 48, on an Elway pass to veteran all-purpose back Steve Sewell, and Elway followed that up with a 12-yard pass to Watson to the Browns 40. Hearts sank in Broncos country when the apparent tying score—an Elway-to-Watson touchdown pass—was just out of bounds on first-and-10 from the Browns 14. But Elway made a great scramble to get to the Browns 5 on second down, setting up the third-and-one pass to Jackson, on a route called "Option Left 62 Rebel."

What everybody forgets about The Drive is that it did not win the game. There was still the matter of Karlis's kicking the extra point—not easy on the freezing, biscuit-strewn turf, in front of the Dawg Pound. Karlis put it through the uprights, but The Drive would have been largely forgotten if the Browns went on to win the game in overtime.

Cleveland seemed to have the advantage in OT, as the Browns won the coin toss and got the ball first.

"This is the Browns' period," Schottenheimer told his team, trying to rally them out of the shell-shocking last drive.

But despite the Browns having decent field position, at their 30, Denver's pumped-up defense limited Kosar to a three-and-out series, with Mecklenburg and Rulon Jones combining to make a big no-gain tackle on Browns running back Herman Fontenot on third-and-two, forcing the Browns to punt and giving the ball back to Elway. This is when the Dawg Pound started to get plenty scared. Their fears were on solid foundation.

The Broncos got their ball on their own 25—paradise of a field position considering their last drive. Playing in a uniform with mud caked down its right side, Elway had little trouble slicing through the Browns again. He hit tight end Orson Mobley with a 20-yard pass on second down, to the Browns 48, but faced his only trouble when the Browns forced a third-and-12.

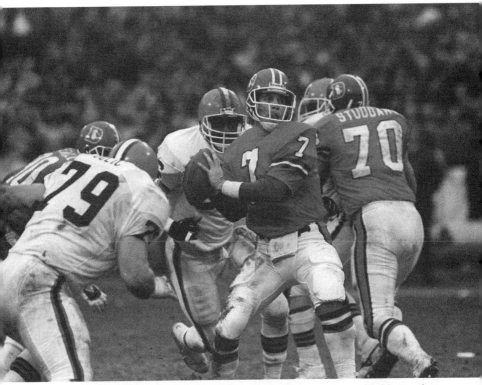

John Elway prepares to hurl the ball downfield en route to a 23–20 overtime victory against the Cleveland Browns in the 1987 AFC Championship Game in Cleveland.

The Browns got a good rush on Elway, but he scrambled away to the left side and hit Watson with a pass on the run, to the Browns 22. The Broncos ran three more plays to the Browns 16.

As Karlis came onto the field, a hyper Elway yelled, "It's just like practice, it's just like practice," for encouragement. Not quite. Having to kick with a bare foot, with dog biscuits everywhere, the temperature below zero, and a crowd howling in derision—all with a trip to the Super Bowl on the line—is not exactly how Karlis grew up practicing his kicks.

"I kind of glanced at John and said, 'Yeah, right,'" Karlis recalls. "I was mainly just concerned with getting good footing on the kick and clearing the dog bones away. But, yes, I felt a little pressure on that kick!"

Elway and Watson were so nervous, they couldn't look. When the ball left Karlis's foot, it appeared the game would continue on. Karlis hooked it left and was immediately worried a slight breeze would carry it wide of the goal post. Goal posts then were not as high as they are today, and the ball was lifted higher than the post on its initial ascent. The only replays of the kick today make it appear debatable if the ball snuck inside the left upright, but only die-hard Browns fans might give the argument. The ball did appear to sneak just inside the post, and Karlis was mobbed.

Ryan was the first to inform Elway and Watson, "We're going to the Super Bowl, boys."

The Broncos received bomb threats from some foolish Browns fans after the game and had to have their airplane searched. But nothing could douse the joy of the day when the legend of Elway truly began—all with a miracle finish.

The Drive, Play by Play
98½ yards; Time of Possession: 4:55
1. Elway, five-yard pass to Winder to Broncos 7
2. Winder, three-yard run to Broncos 10
3. Winder, two-yard run to Broncos 12
4. Winder, three-yard run to Broncos 15
5. Elway, 11-yard run to Broncos 26
6. Elway, 22-yard pass to Sewell to Broncos 48
7. Elway, 12-yard pass to Watson to Browns 40
8. Elway, incomplete pass
9. Elway, eight-yard sack to Browns 48
10. Elway, 20-yard pass to Jackson to Browns 28
11. Elway, incomplete pass
12. Elway, 14-yard pass to Sewell to Browns 14
13. Elway, incomplete pass
14. Elway, nine-yard run to Browns 5
15. Elway, five-yard TD pass to Jackson
    (Karlis kick)

[WEDDING] PARTY TIME FOR ELWAY

In 1993, the Broncos played in Green Bay, losing 30–27 to the Packers. Prior to the game, at the team's hotel in Appleton, Wisconsin, John Elway got into an elevator on his way to a team meeting. In the elevator was the bridesmaid to a wedding in the hotel. She immediately recognized the Broncos quarterback and had no hesitation in making a request: please come greet the bride and groom. Sorry, Elway said. Got a meeting. Give them my best wishes. But a few minutes later, after he stepped out of the elevator, Elway was overcome by guilt. He got back in the elevator, found out where the wedding party was, and gave the happy couple some pictures they no doubt enlarged in their photo album.

SUPER BOWL XXIII—WHAT A WAY TO GO OUT

Who would have believed this? John Elway and the Broncos, defending Super Bowl champions, going for two straight, against an NFC team coached by Dan Reeves?

Reeves used to be the good guy around Denver. But he never did win the big one with the Broncos, including three attempts with Elway as his QB. How awful would this be, if Reeves got his first title as a coach against the Broncos, in what many believed would be Elway's last game? It didn't happen. Not even close. The Broncos, at Pro Player Stadium in Miami, crushed Reeves's Atlanta Falcons, 34–19. And who was the MVP when it was over—with the fourth-most passing yards in Super Bowl history?

Elway, of course. In what would be his last game as a player, the Duke of Denver completed 18 of 29 passes for 336 yards and one touchdown—an 80-yard bomb to Rod Smith. For Elway defenders in his long-simmering feud with Reeves, January 31, 1999, was a day of vindication. If only Reeves had let Elway throw the ball as much as he wanted in those 1980s and early '90s years, they said, Reeves wouldn't still have been looking for his first Super Bowl ring as a coach in Miami. And Elway would have had more than the two he eventually won.

Still, nobody on the Denver side was mourning the past on this day. The Broncos were heavily favored to win, and they did, capping a fantastic, wire-to-wire, 14–2 regular season. The Denver offense was unbelievable, led by Elway and Terrell Davis.

Davis ran for 2,008 yards on 392 carries—a 5.1 average. Denver led the AFC with 501 points, and receiver Smith caught 86 passes for 1,222 yards.

The big game was no different, although it took a while for things to be decided. It was still a game entering the fourth quarter, with Denver up 17–6. But three minutes into the fourth, it was over. Touchdown runs by Howard Griffith and Elway made it 31–6. Game over. Unlike the Broncos' first Super Bowl win a year earlier, there was no nail biting in the final minutes. The entire fourth quarter was a party, with everybody starting to throw the word "*dynasty*" around. "Move over, Carringtons and Mings. There's a new Dynasty in Denver and the free world," wrote *Denver Post* columnist Woody Paige. "The Broncos have won more games (46) in three seasons than any other team in NFL history—17 of which came this year. They are the best, better than all the rest, from the Atlantic (1999) to the Pacific (1998). And they have won the last two Super Bowls to be played in the eventful '90s.

"Hotlanta? NOTLANTA? The Dirty, Stinking Birds were at the bottom of the feud chain. Was it the FarewElway? Let's hope not. The Duke could become the King if he won a third straight. He is John 2:16. Two Super Bowl victories in 16 seasons. And he may very well come back for another."

It didn't happen. Despite the pleas of Bronco Nation, the win in Miami would be it for Elway. After Paige broke the story of Elway's retirement for the *Post*, Elway held a teary press conference on May 2, 1999, at the Inverness Hotel and Golf Club in suburban Denver in which he simply said, "I can't play football anymore."

Gimpy knees were the biggest reason Elway felt he couldn't go on, but there is no question the back-to-back Super Bowl titles had given him the self-satisfaction that contributed to his wanting to go out on top. Later, Elway admitted that if he hadn't won either of his fifth and sixth Super Bowl appearances, "I would have kept playing." The Broncos honored Elway with a retirement ceremony at Mile High Stadium on opening night of the 1999 season shortly after his official announcement. Elway told the crowd, "I love you," and the feeling was definitely mutual. Everybody kept hoping he would change his mind at the last minute, be so overwhelmed by the crowd's chant of "One more year" that he would somehow say, "You know what, to hell with retirement, let's do it again!"

But it didn't happen. And, really, who could blame him? His knees truly were banged up. Just watching him walk was proof enough of that. He'd battled many other injuries, including a ruptured biceps muscle the year before, in which the muscle literally sank to the bottom of his arm.

Still, it seemed so hard to believe at the time: John Elway would no longer be quarterback of the Broncos.

Come again?

"It was tough to see John go, but on the other hand, you felt so good inside, knowing that his career was so complete now, that he didn't have to answer those questions ever again, about not winning a Super Bowl," said Broncos offensive lineman Mark Schlereth, who would play another two years for Denver. "I think it's every player's dream to win the last game you ever play as a pro, and John got to do that. To me, as his teammate, that still feels good to say."

One of the enduring images of Super Bowl XXIII was Schlereth's embrace of Elway in the end zone, after his three-yard run that made the score 31–6 early in the fourth quarter. Elway's familiar, toothy smile, combined with Schlereth's man-hug on the turf, made for the final, feel-good moment of his career.

Fortunately, there was no trash talking done by any of the Broncos after they beat Reeves—or vice versa. Both sides took the classy route, with Reeves congratulating his former QB—the first pro coach Elway ever had. Broncos coach Mike Shanahan, fired by Reeves a few years earlier over differences in offensive philosophy, also shook hands and forgot some testy words between the two earlier in the week. Elway knew he'd had a blessed career after all, which included Reeves's help. The frustration of not winning the big one no doubt caused him to lash out at Reeves in their later, darker years together. He called his last years under Reeves "hell" and Reeves, coaching the New York Giants at the time, responded that it wasn't "heaven" for him, either.

By the first day of February 1999, however, that was forgotten and Elway's name had long since been disassociated with big-game failure. The only thing left to call him now was back-to-back world champion.

UNFORGETTABLE: THAT'S WHAT THEY WERE

BILL ROMANOWSKI: DRUG STORE BRONCO

Bill Romanowski was a pharmacy on cleats. Probably no player in the history of the NFL took—or will take—as many prescription medications, over-the-counter herbal supplements, or other far-out technological medical regimens to improve his performance than the former Boston College Eagle.

Part of Romanowski's intake smorgasbord included steroids and human growth hormone, which he detailed in his autobiography, *Romo: My Life on the Edge—Living Dreams and Slaying Dragons*. It stained his reputation forever in the minds of many, and probably will cost him any shot at induction into the Pro Football Hall of Fame. But, on the field at least, Romanowski was one of the best linebackers of his time, a three-time Super Bowl champion known for his incredible durability in a 16-year career.

Unfortunate or not—and one would wonder why he'd feel it unfortunate if he wrote a tell-all book about it—Romanowski's performance-enhancing substances will probably be what he is most remembered for. And that's a shame. Because Romanowski, whatever one wanted to call him, was a gamer who loved to play.

"He was a guy who came to play every Sunday and gave it all he had," Broncos coach Mike Shanahan said. "He helped our football team become a winner."

A charged-up Bill Romanowski celebrates after sacking Atlanta quarterback Chris Chandler on the opening drive of Super Bowl XXXIII.

In 2003, with the Oakland Raiders in the final year of his career, Romanowski was caught by the NFL using the designer steroid THG and was suspended.

In his book, and on the CBS program *60 Minutes*, Romanowski said he took steroids and HGH only beginning in 2001—which contradicted the words of some former teammates, who said he started in 1995. Victor Conte, founder of the controversial sports nutrition center Bay Area Laboratory Co-Operative, testified to the federal government—after his involvement with baseball star Barry Bonds and others exploded in the media—that Romanowski was the first athlete he ever supplied with steroids.

On his *60 Minutes* interview, Romanowski said he was asked by his son whether he'd ever used drugs.

"Daddy did a lot of things to deal with the pain of the game," Romanowski said he told him.

"Romo," who always wore thick, black eye shade and a sneer on the field, was despised by opponents. But that was all part of his act; Romanowski talked lots of trash, trying to get opponents off their games mentally. He was very similar to a hockey villain named Claude Lemieux, and it was no coincidence that the two became fast friends when Romanowski was a Bronco and Lemieux played for the NHL's Colorado Avalanche.

Occasionally, Romanowski would lash out physically as well, landing him some hefty fines from the NFL. One of his most controversial years with Denver was 1997, when he made national headlines for some on-field activities. The most controversial moment came on December 15 of that year, when he spit in the face of San Francisco receiver J.J. Stokes—a black man. The incident was portrayed in racial terms by some in the press, and Romanowski was fined $7,500 by the league. It became a huge off-field distraction for a team that was 11–4 at the time and a favorite to win a Super Bowl. Romanowski was even criticized publicly by some of his own teammates, including the always-quotable tight end, Shannon Sharpe.

Fortunately for Romanowski, quarterback John Elway came to his aid. In a locker-room meeting, Elway told his teammates to let the incident go, that Romanowski had said he was sorry and let that be the end of it. Nobody was going to say anything back to Elway, and it diffused the situation internally. Denver went on to win the Super Bowl for the first time, with Romanowski having an excellent playoff run. He didn't let the Stokes incident—or a previous fine of $20,000 that year for a hit on Panthers QB Kerry Collins—keep him from engaging in more trash talk. In the AFC championship game at Pittsburgh, Romanowski lit into black Steelers QB Kordell Stewart, who was a favorite in Colorado for playing for the University of Colorado Buffaloes. Romanowski taunted Stewart after he threw an interception, getting right in his face. Teammates usually hate such antics—and no doubt many of Romanowski's did at the time—but Denver went on to win 24–21.

111

SALUTE THAT

If you were in Denver in 1997, you might have thought everyone was in the military. People went around saluting each other all day, in the formal style reserved for commanding officers. Blame Terrell Davis for that. The Broncos star, whose family had a few military connections growing up among the naval bases of San Diego, began a trend that caught on not only in Denver but many other places in pro sports as well.

After scoring touchdowns, Davis began the habit of saluting a teammate or fans. Before long, every player who scored a touchdown for the Broncos was doing it. Mile High Stadium fans, in unison, did it back. By the start of the 1997 playoffs, "Salute That!" fever was in full effect. That, in fact, was the headline in the Rocky Mountain News after the team won its first Super Bowl, in San Diego. The "Mile High Salute" became, for a team, as identified with Colorado as Rocky Mountain Oysters and posh ski resorts. Davis, who loved kids, started the Terrell Davis Salute for Kids Foundation in Denver and San Diego, donating thousands of dollars to the cause.

Kids loved Davis maybe as much as any Bronco who ever played, perhaps because he still wore braces as a young player and because of his wide, bright smile.

After Davis popularized the salute, other pro athletes copied it. Hockey star Jaromir Jagr, for one, began saluting after scoring goals. Davis's move didn't always sit well with the button-down NFL front-office types, however. Celebration penalties were common in the "No Fun League," but Davis never lingered long over his accomplishments. Most of the time, he just did the quick salute and handed the ball to the referee. As the saying goes, Davis looked "like he'd been there before."

In 1999, Romanowski was a four-time world champion and standout player, but his final years were a messy soap opera. In 2001, after a lengthy criminal investigation, he was acquitted by a Denver court of illegally obtaining prescription drugs. He left the Broncos for the hated Raiders after the 2001 season, and it was in Oakland where the big trouble started. In 2003, he was ordered by a court to pay Raiders teammate Marcus Williams a combined

$340,000 for lost wages and medical bills, after he punched Williams in the face during a practice. Then came the failed drug test with the NFL, and, finally, some injuries became too much to bear. Not even his cabinet full of drugs—many of them natural—could ward off the pain anymore. That year, he regretfully retired from football. Two years later, he confessed all of his deeds—proper or otherwise—in his book.

"Do the steroids taint his career? Certainly they taint a little," former Broncos teammate Mark Schlereth said. "His work ethic and longevity were unbelievable, but now you wonder how much of it was due to the 'roids. But, Bill was a good teammate. He always showed up on Sunday, always played hard. There were several times when I was really hurting and Bill would send over one of his gurus. They'd come over and say, 'Bill sent me over here to work on your back or your knee.' So, I appreciated those things."

Romanowski received immunity from prosecutors in the grand jury trial of Conte, and, while admitting to receiving steroids from Conte, he said he took more natural substances than anything synthetic. He used a hyperbaric chamber, took Chinese herbal medicines, ingested something called Bach Flowers, and said he even considered drinking his own urine for possible health benefits (he didn't; even that was too much for Romo).

Romanowski estimates he had as many as 20 concussions in his career, but he credited his vast dietary creativity and fitness curiosity for allowing him to play as long as he did.

If Broncos fans today have a sour memory of Romanowski, they probably are overlooking the times they gleefully cheered him on during his colorful stay in Denver (1996–2001).

Romanowski was the perfect example of the player you loved when he was on your side and hated his guts when he wasn't.

LYLE ALZADO: TRAGIC WARRIOR

Part of what made the Broncos so colorful in the mid-1970s—and not just because of the hue of their uniforms—was in the person of defensive end Lyle Alzado.

Brash, boastful, fiery, abusive, violent, profane, intelligent, warm, funny, and caring—Alzado was all these things and more. A future teammate of Alzado's with the Los Angeles Raiders, Greg Townsend, told a television biographer that Alzado had "a split personality." In fact, his Raiders teammates teased him with nicknames of "Sybil" and "Three Mile Lyle"—you never knew when he'd have a meltdown.

Alzado did everything in extremes. He talked louder than anybody. Ate more than anybody. Hit harder than anybody. Said more outrageous things than anybody. And, unfortunately it would be shown, may have done more harm to his body with performance-enhancing drugs than anybody.

When Alzado died on May 14, 1992, from what the coroner listed as complications from brain cancer, he was known to most Americans already as a cautionary tale. In July 1991, in a first-person story for *Sports Illustrated* titled "I Lied," Alzado admitted to years of steroid abuse, along with use of the controversial human growth hormone. Don't do it, was Alzado's dying message to kids, about the dangers of steroids.

But the cold, hard fact is that without them, Alzado probably never would have been the player he was for 15 NFL seasons. Just an average lineman for his Lawrence, New York, high school team, Alzado was deemed not good enough even to make a junior college team by one coach.

But Alzado was never a quitter, and he convinced the coaching staff of tiny Yankton College in South Dakota, an NAIA school, to take a flyer on him. It was there that Alzado first used steroids, in 1969, and his play immediately changed. He suddenly had the speed and strength to plow past offensive linemen and get to quarterbacks. Pro scouts took notice, and the Broncos selected Alzado in the fourth round of the 1971 draft.

Not about to stop using steroids now at the NFL level, Alzado pushed himself to the limit to try to be the best at his position. In 1977, the magical "Orange Crush" season, he was. That year, he was named the AFC Defensive Player of the Year after leading the Broncos with eight sacks. In Denver's Super Bowl loss to

Dallas, Alzado still managed two sacks of Hall of Famer Roger Staubach.

On the field, steroids helped the bearded, bushy-haired Alzado shine. Off the field, there were concessions. Already with a short temper from a tough childhood, Alzado went into a rage at the slightest confrontation, probably fueled in part by the drugs. If somebody cut him off on the highway, he'd chase down the offender for miles, weaving in and out of traffic. If somebody looked at him the wrong way in a bar, Alzado got right in his face. And, sadly, at least one of his former wives (he was married four times in all) accused him of physical abuse on multiple occasions.

Alzado was wild and crazy, and he reveled in an outlaw image. "I don't really trust a sane person," he once said.

Still, fans of his teams loved him. Alzado was beloved by the Broncos fans, mostly because of his tremendous play. But Coloradans loved his Brooklyn accent, his take-no-guff persona, and his slavish devotion to winning. Sportswriters loved his quick wit, surprising intelligence, and penchant for self-promotion, which made for good copy. Say what you want about Alzado in the end, but he was never, ever dull.

And he was never the big, bad bully he seemed. Alzado loved kids, particularly those with handicaps or tough financial situations. He spent dozens of hours visiting Children's Hospital of Denver, popping in unannounced to hand out candy and toys to sick kids. In 1977, he was given the Byron "Whizzer" White Man of the Year award by the NFL Players' Association for his numerous charitable works. In his career, he raised an estimated $10 million for his causes.

Alzado's career in Denver ended when he was traded to Cleveland in 1979 for an eighth-round draft pick. He had a contract dispute with the Broncos following the 1978 season, feeling he should be the top-paid defensive lineman in the league. After three seasons in Cleveland, he was traded to Los Angeles, where his career enjoyed a rebirth. He was a regular on the Raiders' 1983 Super Bowl team before retiring in 1985.

Always seeking the limelight, Alzado became a part-time actor after going to L.A. He made 15 mostly forgettable movies, but he

Lyle Alzado takes a break during practice in November 1977.

was a sought-after personality for commercials and other business ventures.

Never shy to take risks, Alzado shocked the world in the summer of 1979 when he entered the boxing ring with none other than Muhammad Ali, at Mile High Stadium. While in the midst of his contract dispute with the Broncos, Alzado, a former Golden Gloves boxer, was lured into the ring with the great Ali by promoters looking for a fast buck.

In preparation for the exhibition fight, Alzado sparred in downtown Denver's Skyline Plaza, with radio announcer Larry Zimmer calling the blows and Broncos coach Red Miller acting as referee. At the weigh-in ceremonies at a Denver hotel, things got a little out of hand, with security people having to break up Ali and Alzado. Nobody knew for sure if it had all been staged or not. With Alzado's temper, one never knew for sure about anything.

Alzado ended up going four rounds with Ali in front of a big crowd at Mile High. Ali mostly toyed with Alzado, but his performance against the Champ apparently lured him into thinking he could make a go of it as a pro boxer. He told the Broncos if they didn't meet his contract demands, he'd quit to be a fighter. The ultimatum backfired, with Denver shuffling him off to a bad Cleveland team.

That he finished his career with the hated Raiders and tarnished his reputation with the steroid abuse made him an object of scorn for a later generation of Broncos fans. But for the ones who watched every game from 1971 to 1978, Alzado will always occupy a special place in their thoughts.

SHANNON SHARPE: IF ONLY HE CAME OUT OF HIS SHELL

One year, a shaggy-haired reporter with the *Rocky Mountain News* named Tony Jackson walked into the Broncos locker room, hoping to get a few words with tight end Shannon Sharpe.

"What's up, Kato?" Sharpe said.

Jackson's hair only vaguely resembled that of the long-locked Kato Kaelin, O.J. Simpson's former, infamous housemate and assistant. That mattered not to Sharpe, who, when he spoke, spoke openly and freely and pretty much called anybody anything he wanted.

Shannon Sharpe brutally ribbed reporters, but he was every media person's dream. He loved to talk, and he was funny and outrageous. He also might be the greatest tight end to ever play in the NFL—a surefire Hall of Famer some day. When he retired in 2003, Sharpe had the most receptions of any tight end in history (815) and had won three Super Bowl rings—two with Denver and one with the Baltimore Ravens.

But Sharpe's mouth was something many football fans most remember, including a sideline dig at the New England Patriots that infuriated their fans.

On November 17, 1996, the Broncos laid it good to the Patriots, beating them 34–8 in Foxboro, Massachusetts. The Patriots would go on to the Super Bowl that season, losing to

Green Bay. But on this day, Sharpe compared them to a team in need of rescue.

"Send in the militia, send in the National Guard, the Broncos are coming. It's a massacre," Sharpe said, into a phone on the Broncos sideline late in the game, with the NFL Films cameras rolling.

Once the clip hit the media, Patriots fans exploded in anger. Calls from New England poured into the Broncos team offices, demanding an apology from Sharpe. They never got one.

Sharpe called it as he saw it, and Patriots fans probably over-reacted. What's the fun of football without a little trash talk? But Sharpe's mouth actually created something of an international incident in 1999.

The two-time defending Super Bowl champion Broncos were in Australia to play the first NFL game ever on the continent, in the "American Bowl" against San Diego. The teams arrived a few days early to promote the game, get some sun, and see the sights. Everybody seemed to have a good time. Everybody, expect one player—Sharpe.

Sharpe said he found Australians "rude" and complained of the 17-hour plane ride to get there and the lack of taxi cabs in Sydney. A typical "spoiled American athlete" some Aussies retorted.

"Shannon Sharpe, have a beer—not a whine," read one banner hanging in the stadium for the exhibition game.

Sharpe did not play in the 20–17 Broncos victory—the first game of any kind since 1983 for which John Elway wasn't on the roster. The team listed Sharpe as being out with a sore ankle. Longtime *Denver Post* columnist Woody Paige said Sharpe was really out with "a serious mouth injury (talking too much)."

Sharpe normally shrugged off personal criticism—or fired back twice as hard verbally. But he took the shots over his Australian comments personally, and he said he would not talk to the Denver media for the rest of the season. And, he didn't. It was a long, long year for the reporters around the team.

After all, imagine not being able to talk to a guy with some memorable lines like these: "We were so poor, a robber once broke

Shannon Sharpe laughs while being interviewed by reporters at Super Bowl XXXIII Media Day activities in Miami on January 26, 1999.

into our house, and we ended up robbing the robber" and "I was a terrible student. I didn't graduate magna cum laude. I graduated, 'Thank you, Lawdy!'"

Sharpe, as they say, walked the walk on the football field—not just talked the talk. Blessed with a big, but sleek, muscular frame, Sharpe might have been the fastest tight end in league history. His brother, Sterling, was an NFL star previously, with Green Bay. Together, they are easily the best brother receiver combination of all time. And the most outspoken pair of brothers ever. Both went on to careers as color analysts with American networks after retiring.

Sharpe was a huge contributor to the Broncos' back-to-back Super Bowl teams, catching five of John Elway's 12 completions in Denver's victory over Green Bay in Super Bowl XXXII. He also made a major, third-down catch to get a first down in Denver's AFC Championship Game victory over Pittsburgh two weeks earlier. That first down effectively ended the game, allowing the

Broncos to run out the clock instead of having to punt it away in a 24–21 game.

Sharpe's best game as a pro might have been in a Broncos playoff loss, to the L.A. Raiders in 1993. He caught 13 passes for 156 yards and a touchdown, tying an NFL postseason record for receptions.

After winning a second championship ring in 1999 with Denver, Sharpe looked to cash in with owner Pat Bowlen and coach/de facto GM Mike Shanahan on a new contract. Shockingly, Sharpe would be wearing the ugly purple uniforms of the Ravens a few months later.

Insulted by the offers from Broncos management, Sharpe looked elsewhere and found a big fan in Ravens GM Ozzie Newsome—himself one of the greatest tight ends in league history. Sharpe accepted an offer from Baltimore, and on December 31, 2000, he exacted his revenge on the Broncos.

It just so happened the Broncos and Ravens met that day in an AFC wild-card playoff game, at PSINet Stadium. And who do you suppose made a 58-yard, Franco Harris–style "Immaculate Reception" touchdown catch against the Broncos that day?

Shannon Sharpe, of course, who grabbed a ball that was tipped in midair by Baltimore's Jamal Lewis and Denver's Terrell Buckley and ran it all the way for six points in the second quarter, making it 14–3 Ravens. Baltimore would go on to win 21–3, but surprisingly Sharpe did not have much to say in the way of trash talk toward the team that spurned him.

Sharpe won his third ring that year with the Ravens and played one more year in Baltimore before re-signing with Denver in 2002. He caught another 123 passes for the Broncos in two more seasons before hanging it up after 2003.

It wasn't long before CBS signed him to a broadcast contract. Finally, Sharpe could make his living with just his mouth.

IN THE CLUTCH

JOHN ELWAY: THE KING OF COMEBACKS

John Elway was a victim of one of the greatest—and most freak-ish—comeback moments in sports history in his last game as a college player. His Stanford team, fresh from an Elway-led score in the last two minutes that gave the Cardinal a lead over the University of California with just seconds left, lost the game after a series of Cal laterals led to a touchdown return on the last kickoff. The game is most remembered for when members of the Stanford band came onto the field during the return, thinking the game was over. Instead, they helped provide inadvertent blocking for the winning Cal touchdown—and kept Stanford from making a bowl game.

As a pro, however, Elway was the king of breaking the hearts of opposing teams in the final minutes. If the Broncos were behind by less than seven points, it didn't matter. As long as Elway had the ball in his hands and any time left on the clock, Broncos fans were still upbeat.

There have been a lot of great "two-minute" quarterbacks in NFL history and a lot of great comebacks. But probably nobody in league history was consistently better in clutch, seemingly impos-sible comeback situations than the Duke of Denver.

"You always knew you had a chance with him on the football field at the end of a game," offensive lineman Mark Schlereth said. "You felt so confident running up to the line of scrimmage. You'd

---

DID YOU KNOW...

That not only did the Broncos have the first starting black quarterback in pro football history, the team had the first black place-kicker as well?

Gene Mingo, a member of the American Football League Hall of Fame, played several positions for Denver from 1960 to 1964. One of them was place-kicker, and his 18-yard field goal on October 2, 1960, against Oakland were the first points ever scored at Mile High Stadium (then called Bears Field).

---

be excited just to see what he'd do this time. And you could see the looks of fear in the eyes of guys across the line."

The numbers are staggering: In a career that spanned from 1983 to 1998, Elway engineered 47 fourth-quarter or overtime, game-saving or game-winning drives for the Broncos. Denver's record in those games: 46–0–1.

Nothing quite matches the shine in Broncos fans' eyes when they remember some of Elway's many comebacks. High on the list, of course, is "The Drive" in Cleveland, in the 1987 AFC Championship Game. But there were so many more Houdini escapes.

Maybe an even better comeback feat than Cleveland '87 was a 26–24 Broncos AFC playoff victory over the Houston Oilers, on January 4, 1992, at Mile High Stadium.

The Oilers, featuring Hall of Fame QB Warren Moon, led the whole game—except for the last 16 seconds. Houston led 24–16 early in the fourth quarter, following an Al Del Greco field goal, and the Oilers defense was doing a good job on Elway's offense much of the day. This was a Broncos team that didn't have a lot on the ground, still relying on Elway and the "Three Amigos" receiving corps of Vance Johnson, Mark Jackson, and Ricky Nattiel.

What made this game so memorable wasn't that Elway was able to overcome an eight-point deficit in the fourth quarter. It was how he did it. Three times, Elway faced fourth down in the final quarter, and on a couple of them he appeared to be a sure sack victim. But all three times, Elway wriggled free and made the plays that kept drives going.

On the first of the fourth downs, a fourth-and-four from the Houston 41 and Denver down the eight points, Elway hit Michael Young with a pass, and he broke two tackles en route to the Houston 15. Denver scored from there to make it 24–23 Houston, and the Oilers were forced to punt the ball back to the Broncos.

But a nice punt by Houston's Greg Montgomery put the ball at the Denver 2-yard line, with 2:07 left. Would it be "The Drive, Part II"?" Yes, it would. But the Broncos needed just a field goal on this one.

What a drive it was, full of madcap, scrambling heroics by Elway. After Young caught a 22-yard pass to get some good breathing room for Elway, Houston allowed just four yards on the next three plays, bringing up a fourth-and-six from the 28. The Oilers got a big pass rush on Elway, driving him out of the pocket toward the left side. One tackle for anything less than the six, and it was over. Houston would move on to the AFC Championship Game in Buffalo. But Elway broke a tackle and staggered toward the first-down marker on the sideline. He barely made it. The crowd, in full roar, rose to its feet. Denver was driving to the South Stands, where fans were stomping their boots in anticipation of Elway's imminent arrival.

Three straight incomplete passes later, however, it was fourth-and-10 from the Broncos 35. The Broncos looked out of miracles. But, O, ye of little faith, this is Elway we're talking about. Houston got another big rush on him, but Elway slipped free from the pocket and looked like he might try to run for the first down again. Other Houston defenders were ready to meet him near the line of scrimmage, however. Elway was about to be hit at the line—or forfeit a chance to pass if he took nearly another step anyway—when he spotted receiver Johnson on the left side. Elway floated a pass off the run that hit Johnson in full stride for a 44-yard completion to the Houston 21 with under a minute left.

Running back Steve Sewell got the Broncos 10 yards closer with a nice run on first down, and two plays later, kicker David Treadwell booted a 28-yard field goal with 16 seconds left. Mile

John Elway flashes the number one sign as he leaves the field following the Broncos' win over the Cleveland Browns in the AFC Championship Game on January 14, 1990.

High went crazy. Houston players could only shake their heads over what Elway had done. He'd been right in their grasp the whole fourth quarter, but he never could be caught.

The fourth-quarter comeback against Houston was one of six in Elway's playoff career, starting with "The Drive" and culminating with the five-play, 49-yard drive that gave Denver a 31–24 lead over Green Bay in Super Bowl XXXII.

The first of all his pro comebacks came on December 11, 1983, against the team that drafted him—the Baltimore Colts. Able to do nothing through three quarters against the Colts, Elway threw three fourth-quarter TD passes to give the Broncos a 21–19 win at Mile High. The last of his career fourth-quarter comebacks was on

December 6, 1998, against Kansas City. The Chiefs led the 12–0 Broncos 31–28 with 6:13 left, but Elway directed a five-play, 50-yard drive, capped off by a 24-yard TD pass to Shannon Sharpe with 2:39 left. The Denver lead held up for a 35–31 win.

"I just liked the ball in my hands with a chance to win the game," Elway said after his retirement. "All you wanted was a chance, and I was lucky to play with a lot of great players who helped make some of those comebacks possible."

JOHN ELWAY'S 47 CAREER FOURTH-QUARTER GAME-SAVING OR GAME-WINNING HEROICS

- December 11, 1983, vs. Baltimore—Elway throws three fourth-quarter TD passes, the last a 26-yarder to Gerald Wilhite with 44 seconds left in a 21–19 Denver win.
- November 4, 1984, vs. New England—Engineers eight-play, 78-yard drive, finishing with seven-yard TD pass to Butch Johnson with 4:03 left, to tie the score, 19–19. Broncos win 26–19 on Dennis Smith's touchdown fumble return.
- November 11, 1984, vs. San Diego—Directs 10-play, 77-yard TD drive, culminating in a one-yard Sammy Winder scoring run with 38 seconds left, for a 16–13 victory.
- December 9, 1984, vs. San Diego—Directs 12-play, 40-yard drive, capped by a Rich Karlis 24-yard field goal with 2:08 left in 16–13 win.
- September 22, 1985, at Atlanta—Overcomes 28–27 deficit with three fourth-quarter scoring drives (two TDs, one FG) in 44–28 win.
- November 11, 1985, vs. San Francisco—Directs nine-play, 63-yard drive, capped by a 24-yard Rich Karlis field goal with 1:27 left in 17–16 win.
- November 17, 1985, vs. San Diego—Directs seven-play, 48-yard drive, capped by 34-yard Rich Karlis field goal with five seconds left to tie game 24–24. Denver wins in overtime on a blocked field goal and 60-yard TD return by Louis Wright.

Super Bowl XXXII quarterbacks and NFL legends Brett Favre and John Elway meet on the field during warm-ups at Qualcomm Stadium on January 25, 1998 in San Diego.

- December 1, 1985, at Pittsburgh—Directs seven-play, 58-yard TD drive, finished with a one-yard Sammy Winder run with 1:45 left to take 24–23 lead. Denver wins 31–23.
- December 14, 1985, vs. Kansas City—Directs eight-play, 59-yard TD drive, capped by a one-yard Sammy Winder run with 22 seconds left in 14–13 victory.
- December 20, 1985, at Seattle—Directs eight-play, 80-yard drive to tie the game, 24–24, with 2:35 remaining. Elway is injured, but Denver wins 27–24 on a Rich Karlis field goal, on a drive led by backup QB Gary Kubiak.
- September 7, 1986, vs. L.A. Raiders—Directs nine-play, 39-yard drive, capped by a seven-yard TD pass to Gene Lang with 5:11 left in a 38–36 win.

- January 11, 1987, at Cleveland (AFC Championship Game)—Directs 15-play, 98-yard drive, capped by a five-yard TD pass to Mark Jackson with 39 seconds left, to tie the game 20–20. Denver wins in OT on Rich Karlis's 33-yard field goal.
- September 20, 1987, at Green Bay—Directs 18-play, 80-yard drive, capped by a one-yard Steve Sewell TD run with 5:53 left to tie the game 17–17. Game ends in an overtime tie.
- November 16, 1987, vs. Chicago—Directs eight-play, 61-yard drive, capped by a four-yard TD run by Steve Sewell with 4:58 left in the 31–29 win.
- December 6, 1987, vs. New England—Directs six-play, 74-yard drive, finished by a two-yard TD pass to Mark Jackson with 12:41 left for 24–20 lead. Denver wins 31–20.
- January 17, 1988, vs. Cleveland (AFC Championship Game)—Directs five-play, 75-yard TD drive, capped by a 20-yard pass to Sammy Winder with 4:01 left for 38–31 lead. Denver wins 38–33.
- October 9, 1988, at San Francisco—Directs nine-play, 58-yard drive, capped by an eight-yard TD pass to Vance Johnson with 8:37 left to tie the game 13–13. Denver wins in OT on a Rich Karlis field goal.
- October 8, 1989, vs. San Diego—Directs 11-play, 74 yard drive, culminating in Bobby Humphrey's 17-yard TD run with 1:03 left in a 16–10 win.
- October 22, 1989, at Seattle—Throws 54-yard TD pass to Vance Johnson (only play of drive) with 2:19 left to tie the game 21–21. Denver wins in OT on a David Treadwell field goal.
- November 12, 1989, at Kansas City—Directs 10-play, 72-yard drive, capped by a 26-yard David Treadwell field goal with 0:01 left in 16–13 win.
- January 7, 1990, vs. Pittsburgh (AFC divisional playoff)—Directs nine-play, 71-yard drive, capped by a one-yard Melvin Bratton run with 2:27 left in 24–23 win.
- September 17, 1990, vs. Kansas City—Directs 10-play, 79-yard drive, finished by a 22-yard David Treadwell field goal with no time left in 24–23 win.

- October 21, 1990, at Indianapolis—Directs nine-play, 58-yard drive, capped by a 42-yard David Treadwell field goal with 3:45 left for 20-17 lead. Denver wins 27-17.
- October 20, 1991, vs. Kansas City—Directs seven-play, 70-yard drive, capped by a 27-yard David Treadwell field goal with 2:37 left in a 19-16 win.
- October 27, 1991, at New England—Directs nine-play, 42-yard drive, capped by a 34-yard David Treadwell field goal with 1:56 left in a 9-6 win.
- December 8, 1991, at Cleveland—Directs 16-play, 64-yard TD drive, capped by a six-yard pass to Vance Johnson with 8:54 left to break the 7-7 tie. Denver wins 17-7.
- December 15, 1991, vs. Phoenix—Directs six-play, 66-yard drive, capped by Elway's four-yard TD run with 1:46 in 24-19 win.
- January 4, 1992, vs. Houston (AFC divisional playoff)—Directs 12-play, 87-yard drive, capped by a 28-yard David Treadwell field goal with 20 seconds left in a 26-24 win.
- September 6, 1992, vs. L.A. Raiders—Directs seven-play, 85-yard drive, capped by Reggie Rivers's one-yard TD run with 55 seconds left in a 17-13 win.
- October 4, 1992, vs. Kansas City—Directs three-play, 27-yard drive, capped by a 12-yard TD pass to Vance Johnson with 38 seconds left in a 20-19 win.
- October 18, 1992, vs. Houston—Directs three-play, 80-yard drive, capped by a 20-yard TD pass to Reggie Rivers with 1:34 left in a 27-21 win.
- December 12, 1993, vs. Kansas City—Directs three-play, 11-yard drive, finished with a six-yard TD pass to Shannon Sharpe with 10:34 left in a 27-21 win.
- October 23, 1994, at San Diego—Directs four-play, four-yard drive leading to a 54-yard field goal by Jason Elam with 10:02 left to put Denver up 17-15. Denver wins 20-15.
- November 20, 1994, vs. Atlanta—Directs 10-play, 73-yard drive, capped by a 32-yard TD pass to Anthony Miller to pull Denver within three points, 28-25, then drove 57 yards on 10 plays, capped by Elway's four-yard TD run with 1:56 left for a 32-28 win.

- September 17, 1995, vs. Washington—Directs eight-play, 80-yard drive, capped by a 43-yard TD pass to Rod Smith with no time remaining in a 38–31 win.
- November 19, 1995, vs. San Diego—Directs seven-play, 53-yard drive, capped by a 32-yard Jason Elam field goal with 3:43 left in a 30–27 win.
- December 24, 1995, at Oakland—Directs 13-play, 87-yard drive, capped by a 13-yard pass to Ed McCaffrey and two-point conversion to tie the game, 28–28, with 5:46 left. Then, directed nine-play, 53-yard drive, capped by Jason Elam's 37-yard field goal with 48 seconds left in a 31–28 win.
- September 15, 1996, vs. Tampa Bay—Directs 14-play, 80-yard drive, capped by a Terrell Davis three-yard TD run with 3:32 left in 27–23 win.

THE FIRST MONDAY NIGHT GAME

In 1973, the Broncos played in front of a national, Monday night audience for the first time.

On October 22, Howard Cosell and his cohorts in yellow ABC blazers came to Mile High Stadium for a game against the Oakland Raiders. Many Broncos fans remember the game vividly, and not just because of Jim Turner's dramatic kick at the final gun that gained a 23–23 tie (there was no overtime in those days).

The city of Denver really hadn't had much national exposure—in anything—until that point. Sure, they'd had professional sports teams and a renowned ski industry and other tourist attractions. But until the ABC cameras came, it seemed as if Denver would forever be just a "dusty old cowtown." The game was a thriller, capped by Turner's 35-yard kick.

"I won a Super Bowl with the Jets and played in the famous 'Heidi' game with the Jets and went to a Super Bowl with the Broncos," Turner said. "But that kick on Monday night is something I'll never forget. It's a top career moment for me."

- October 20, 1996, vs. Baltimore—Directs 10-play, 57-yard drive, capped by a six-yard TD pass to Ed McCaffrey with 10:57 left for 38–34 lead. Denver wins 45–34.
- November 4, 1996, at Oakland—Directs six-play, 73-yard drive, capped by a 49-yard TD pass to Rod Smith 4:14 left for a 22–21 win.
- November 24, 1996, at Minnesota—Directs 11-play, 84-yard drive, finished by a five-yard TD pass to Ed McCaffrey with 19 seconds left for 21–17 win.
- October 26, 1997, at Buffalo—Directs nine-play, 43-yard drive during overtime, setting up a game-winning 33-yard field goal by Jason Elam.
- November 2, 1997, vs. Seattle—Directs eight-play, 69-yard drive, capped by a 22-yard Jason Elam field goal with 7:28 left in a 30–27 win.
- January 4, 1998, at Kansas City (AFC divisional playoff)—Directs six-play, 49-yard drive, capped by a one-yard Terrell Davis TD run with 12:32 left in a 14–10 win.
- January 25, 1998, vs. Green Bay (Super Bowl XXXII)—Directs five-play, 49-yard drive, capped by a one-yard Terrell Davis TD run with 1:45 left in a 31–24 win.
- November 1, 1998, at Cincinnati—Directs five-play, 53-yard drive, capped by a five-yard Terrell Davis TD run with 58 seconds left in a 33–26 win.
- December 6, 1998, vs. Kansas City—Directs five-play, 50-yard drive, capped by a 24-yard TD pass to Shannon Sharpe with 3:34 left in a 35–31 win.

"THESE ARE THE INDIANAPOLIS COLTS"—NOT BY A LONG SHOT

Don't let anybody fool you: when Green Bay Packers quarterback Brett Favre hit receiver Antonio Freeman for a 22-yard touchdown pass four minutes and two seconds into Super Bowl XXXII, there wasn't a Broncos fan anywhere that didn't immediately think this would be anything other than another embarrassing blowout in front of the entire world. Denver went into the perfectly sunny January 25, 1998, Sunday in San Diego 0–4 in Super Bowls, by a combined score of 163–50. The Packers, defending Super Bowl champs, were unbeatable. All the experts said so, including Las Vegas, which listed Denver as a 12-point underdog. In Green Bay, sportswriters heaped derision on the Broncos, calling them the AFC's latest "sacrificial lamb." Poor John Elway, said the media; the bridesmaid of football, the great player who never could win the big one. Denver would be the first team to suffer five Super Bowl losses, surpassing Minnesota and Buffalo for futility.

All the talk of how "this time it would be different," how these Denver Broncos had the true right stuff to win a championship, seemed laughably naïve again when Freeman hauled in Favre's pass, right at the edge of the end zone. Right away, after Green Bay's first possession, it was 7–0. Now the Broncos had been outscored 170–50 in football's biggest game. At least the Vikings and the Bills had made it close once in their four losses.

TOP FIVE

Most Yards on Punt Returns, Regular Season

1. 653—Rick Upchurch, 1977
2. 543—Darrien Gordon, 1997
3. 536—Rick Upchurch, 1976
4. 493—Rick Upchurch, 1978
5. 468—Gerald Wilhite, 1986

"I'm sure there were a lot of fans that immediately sank in their chairs, preparing for the worst," said Broncos offensive lineman Mark Schlereth, who only a few weeks before had undergone the 20th surgery of his career, to repair a herniated disc in his back. "But we knew as a team that we were ready and we certainly hadn't let one early touchdown get us thinking it was over already. We had too good a football team. We were very confident going into the game."

Indeed, the Broncos showed right after Favre's TD pass that this day would ultimately be different. On their first possession of the game, Elway led the Broncos on a 10-play, 58-yard scoring drive, culminating in Terrell Davis's one-yard run, to make it 7–7. Right back at ya, Packers.

"We knew we were going to be able to move the football on them," Schlereth said. "We'd done it all year—we had what is probably one of the top five offenses in NFL history that year—and we knew they weren't going to shut us down. Mike Shanahan just had such a great game plan. We switched our blocking assignments, doing what other teams hadn't done. You look back and you think, 'Was it really that simple? Because, it seemed like stealing at the time against them.'"

Tyrone Braxton intercepted Favre on Green Bay's next possession, and eight plays later, Elway ran a naked bootleg into the end zone. Free safety Steve Atwater forced a Favre fumble on Green Bay's next possession, recovered by lineman Neil Smith at the Packers 33. The Broncos were stuffed on three straight plays, but Jason Elam converted Favre's turnover into three more points, with a 51-yard field goal—second longest in Super Bowl history.

Mark Chmura caught a TD pass from Favre right before halftime to cut Denver's lead to 17–14. But the Broncos went into the locker room ahead at the half for the first time in their five Super Bowls. Victory—unimaginable, sweet victory—was 30 minutes away. It would be a long, excruciating 30 minutes. The second half would go down as one of the most exciting in NFL history, a true nail-biter with great plays on both sides.

One needed only to look at Elway's father, Jack, to see how nerve-wracking the second half was for Broncos fans. Sitting in the press box, Jack Elway was a mess. He could not watch some of the time, biting his nails, burying his face before big third-down plays. Broncos fans went into the extended halftime fretting about not only the fate of the second half but also the fate of star running back Davis. In the second quarter, Davis suddenly got a

---

DID YOU KNOW...

That in 2005 the Broncos became the first team in NFL history to have two 100-yard rushers and a 300-yard passer in the same game?

On October 30, 2005, against Philadelphia, Mike Anderson (126 yards) and Tatum Bell (107) ran for at least 100, while QB Jake Plummer threw for 309 yards.

migraine headache—a chronic problem in his life that hadn't surfaced all season. Of course, on Super Bowl Sunday, it did. The Broncos would have to play the rest of game without the NFL's most valuable player, it seemed. Typical Broncos luck.

But Davis showed his heart by going into the game, on coach Mike Shanahan's plea, to act as a decoy on Elway's TD run that made it 14–7. Davis's presence, Shanahan correctly foresaw, was the only way the Packers might be fooled on a bootleg run. Despite having blurry vision and pounding pain in his temples, Davis trudged into the huddle and took a fake handoff from Elway, which sent all the Packers defenders the wrong way, toward Davis, clearing the way for Elway to waltz into the end zone.

The long halftime, with 30-second commercials costing $1.3 million a pop and acts such as the Four Tops, the Temptations, and Boyz II Men serving as entertainment, allowed Davis more time to recover from the migraine. Davis was late taking his medication—Migranal—which he'd used all season to control his headaches. The excitement of playing in his hometown, and all the lights and pageantry, might have contributed to a headache kicking in normally by the start of the game. But when he was tripped up on a run and hit his head against the leg of a Packers defender in the first quarter, it brought on symptoms that worsened to extreme conditions by the half.

Davis, who considered suicide as a child because of the headaches, wrote for SuperBowl.com about his memories of the event:

> I was thinking, 'Not this time, not on this day.' I had stayed in for a couple of plays, not wanting to tell anyone about it. But I knew I couldn't keep playing like this. I finally told the head trainer, Steve Antonopulos (we all call him "Greek") about what was going on, and he sat me down on the bench. He gave me some medication, and went to tell [Shanahan] what was happening. Mike told Greek to take me into the locker room now and to just keep me there before halftime, so we went to the locker room. I sat there with a towel around my head, trying to

recover in a dark, cool place, and the only sound I could hear was the game on TV. Halftime came, and the players started coming back in. By then, my vision was clearing up, and with the extended Super Bowl halftime, I found I was ready to go back out for the second half.

Davis would have a half that would put his name on the Most Valuable Player trophy. The roller-coaster half began with a seven-play, 17-yard drive that ended in Packers kicker Ryan Longwell's 27-yard, tying field goal. That made 10 straight points by the Packers, and the nacho cheese and buffalo wings in the stomach pits of Broncos fans started to feel more indigestible than normal. The Broncos would crush their fans again, no doubt. They would become the Boston Red Sox of football—the first five-time Super Bowl losers.

Or, as Packers safety Eugene Robinson said, "the Indianapolis Colts." With the Broncos moving the ball better than expected against a Packers defense featuring Robinson and standouts such as Reggie White and Gilbert Brown, Robinson tried to fire up his teammates by comparing the Broncos to the lowly Colts.

"These are the Indianapolis Colts," Robinson barked on the sideline. "The Indianapolis Colts!"

As motivation ploys go, Robinson's was a lead balloon. The Indianapolis Colts? With certain Hall of Famers such as Elway, Shannon Sharpe, and Gary Zimmerman, and possible ones such as Davis, Elam, Treadwell, Bill Romanowski, and Rod Smith? Hardly.

Still, it looked like all those Hall of Famers would blow it for Broncos fans, especially when Robinson—yes, him—intercepted Elway on the first play after Broncos veteran Tim McKyer recovered a fumbled kickoff following Davis's one-yard TD run that made it 24–17. The Packers went 85 yards on four plays following Elway's gaffe, tying the game and leaving everybody in Colorado assuming the worst was ahead. But these Broncos truly were different.

Those would be the final points the Broncos defense would allow. Elway, meanwhile, went from a three-time Super Bowl loser

CHAMP'S RUN TO (ALMOST) GLORY

One of the best-remembered plays in recent Broncos history was Champ Bailey's 100-yard interception return of Tom Brady that helped beat the two-time defending Super Bowl champion New England Patriots in a 2006 playoff game.

Even though the return was officially recorded as 100 yards, Bailey did not score on the play. He tired and was tackled right before the goal line by New England's Benjamin Watson, fumbling the ball.

Bailey's play turned a potential go-ahead score by the Patriots into a subsequent Broncos TD that gave Denver a 17–6 lead entering the fourth quarter. The Broncos would win 27–13, and Bailey got the game ball from coach Mike Shanahan.

and thrower of that ghastly interception into the legend he remains today with a brilliant show of leadership.

His final statistics (12–22, 123 yards, no touchdowns, one interception) were not legendary. But one earlier play, prior to the interception, put Elway into the Legends Pantheon. On a third-and-six from the Packers 12, Elway scrambled for the first down and was nailed by Robinson and LeRoy Butler at the 6. The hit sent Elway spinning 360 degrees, but not only did he hold on to the football, he also got the first down. He came up, throwing his fist in the air, and Davis punctuated the drive with the TD run and Mile High Salute that gave the Broncos the 24–17 lead. After the interception and tying Packers score, Elway led Denver on a five-play, 49-yard scoring drive—again capped by Davis's one-yard run—that would be the game's deciding score. The Packers didn't even try to stop Davis on the scoring run, conceding it to get the ball back faster. The Denver defense had to hold Favre one last time, and they had to do it on a fourth-down play without Atwater and Ray Crockett, who collided hard with each other breaking up a third-down pass.

But on fourth down, linebacker John Mobley ended 38 years of championship frustration, when he knocked down Favre's pass.

That was it, but nobody at first seemed to believe it. Elway's eyes didn't appear to register at first after Mobley knocked down the pass. When they did, he leaped into the air, throwing his fist, flashing his famous buck teeth. All he had to do now was run out the clock, which he did by kneeling down at the 30-yard line.

"Oh baby, they're gonna win this thing!" Broncos play-by-play man Dave Logan shouted into his radio microphone.

The Broncos—finally!—were Super Bowl champions. Davis, with 157 yards on 30 carries and three touchdowns, was the easy choice as MVP. Denver went crazy. Federal Boulevard, adjacent to Mile High Stadium, was engulfed with honking cars. Revelers flowed into lower downtown Denver, waving index fingers, to the requisite blaring of Queen's "We Are the Champions." Four thousand other fans celebrated inside McNichols Sports Arena, watching on a big screen. On the Qualcomm Stadium turf where it all happened, Broncos owner Pat Bowlen handed the Vince Lombardi Trophy over to Elway, telling the world, "This one's for John."

Final score: Denver 31, Green Bay 24.

Wrote *Denver Post* Broncos writer Adam Schefter: "They tore apart history and wrote their own. For the first time in 38 years, for the first time ever, the Denver Broncos are masters of the football universe. World champions. It has a ring to it."

"It still doesn't seem real sometimes," Broncos receiver Rod Smith said, years later. "That whole day seems like a dream. A really, really good dream."

ED MCCAFFREY: HOW DID HE HOLD ON?

Ed McCaffrey was like a cartoon character when he played football. Like Wile E. Coyote, he'd have any number of seemingly fatal collisions and still just bounce back up once the stars cleared over his head.

McCaffrey was a dichotomy. He looked a little too pretty and spoke in too many complete sentences to fit the mold of perhaps the toughest receiver of his time. But beneath the good looks and the Stanford education was a steel-town toughness. McCaffrey

Ed McCaffrey makes another improbable-looking catch against the San Diego Chargers in 2000.

was born in Waynesboro, Pennsylvania, an old industrial town known for its machine shops and not much else. He played high school football in nearby Allentown, another hardscrabble city, where football was one of the main diversions for the locals.

McCaffrey's Allentown Central Catholic High School played in the ultracompetitive Lehigh Valley Conference, where previous NFL alumni included Chuck Bednarik and Matt Millen—two of the meanest, toughest players who ever played.

In the Lehigh Valley Conference, you were a wimp if you left a game with an injury. It was there that McCaffrey learned to get back up, no matter how hard he got hit. That applied in the metaphorical sense as well; life's setbacks were no reason to get down and depressed. What mattered was overcoming them, learning from them. McCaffrey's tale is not a "Rudy" or "Rocky" one, however. He was highly recruited out of high school as a wide receiver, eventually selecting Stanford, where somebody named John Elway once played. He was an All-American with the Cardinal and was drafted 83rd overall by the New York Giants in 1991.

This was when McCaffrey's story did turn into more of a rags-to-riches one. McCaffrey led the 1992 Giants in catches under coach Ray Handley, but Handley was fired and replaced by former

Broncos coach Dan Reeves. McCaffrey slipped on Reeves's depth chart, and by the end of 1993, he was released.

McCaffrey caught on with the San Francisco 49ers, but he didn't catch much else. He had just 11 receptions in 16 games in 1994, and his career seemed in big trouble. He was again cut, but former 49ers offensive coordinator Mike Shanahan thought highly of McCaffrey and extended a training-camp invitation in 1995, in his first year as head coach of the Broncos.

TOP FIVE

Most Postseason Receptions in Broncos History

1. 49—Rod Smith
2. 47—Shannon Sharpe
3. 41—Vance Johnson
4. 36—Ed McCaffrey
5. 31—Steve Sewell

Slowly but surely, McCaffrey rebuilt his career. By 1997, it took off. He was a vital member of the Broncos' first Super Bowl–winning team, making some huge catches in the playoffs. One of them was a 43-yard reception to the 1-yard line against Kansas City in an AFC divisional game at Arrowhead Stadium. That led to Terrell Davis's touchdown run that was the difference in the Broncos' 14–10 victory. In the Super Bowl against Green Bay, McCaffrey caught two passes for 45 yards, but his most memorable moment probably was a crushing block he made against the Packers' Brian Williams. On what proved the Broncos' game-winning touchdown drive in the fourth quarter, Elway hit Howard Griffith with a pass that looked to be for just a short gain, with Williams closing in. But McCaffrey freed Griffith for the bulk of his 23-yard gain with a massive block, which Williams never saw coming. With Williams down, McCaffrey stood over him like Cassius Clay over Sonny Liston, giving a stern finger point as an exclamation. McCaffrey, however, took many more of those kinds of hits than he administered. Because he had no fear of running over the middle, he exposed himself to big hits—and defenders obliged.

One of the hardest came on September 10, 2001, at Invesco Field at Mile High—the first regular-season game ever played in the new stadium. Against the New York Giants, McCaffrey caught another pass over the middle for good yardage, from quarterback Brian Griese. Giants defender Sean Williams made a huge hit, but, as usual, McCaffrey held on to the football.

McCaffrey stayed down for a few seconds, which also was normal to Broncos fans. Many times over the years, "Eddie Mac" had stayed down for a bit after taking a blow. This time, however, things weren't normal. McCaffrey didn't get up. This time, he'd suffered a broken leg—broken in two places.

Coming off a career-high, 101-reception season in 2000, McCaffrey was a bona fide NFL star by then, and one of the Broncos' most popular players. His smiling face seemed to be everywhere, pitching everything from his own line of mustard to vision correction companies.

But now, his career was over. It had to be, right? How many wide receivers resumed a career after breaking a leg in two places? McCaffrey did. He missed the rest of the 2001 season, and many didn't think he would ever play again. It was a complete fracture in the leg, requiring extensive surgery. The rehabilitation was going to be long and grueling, but McCaffrey was no quitter. He worked at it all day, every day for nearly a year, pushing himself to exhaustion. But it paid off when he was pronounced healthy enough to play in 2002. McCaffrey had a great year, catching 69 passes for 903 yards. He might have lost a little speed, but he still had great hands and his courage over the middle was no less. He still took some major blows, but nothing would ever knock him out of a game again. Yet, surprisingly, McCaffrey was out of the league just a year later. He started just seven games in 2003, hurt by groin and concussion injuries, and was pushed down on the depth chart by the emergence of rookie Ashley Lelie. McCaffrey also didn't seem to have the kind of chemistry with new QB Jake Plummer that he'd had with Elway and Griese. He caught only 19 passes for the season, at the end of which he was 35 years old. He might have been the youngest-looking 35-year-old in the league, but the NFL is a very unforgiving place for anyone near that age.

McCaffrey retired on March 1, 2004. Shanahan gave him the ultimate compliment by calling him "the most complete player" he'd ever coached. McCaffrey had some of the best receiving seasons in NFL history, but he admitted that might not be what he's most remembered for. "No receiver in the NFL wants to be remembered for how many times they got hit hard," he told reporters on retirement day. "Speed, great hands, scoring touchdowns—but not getting crushed. But, hey, at least people will remember me. That's the only way I knew how to play the game."

15 MINUTES (OR A LITTLE LONGER) OF FAME

A STAR, IF ONLY BRIEFLY

Joe Dudek knows what it feels like to have your face on the cover of *Sports Illustrated*. He knows what it's like to have all of Mile High Stadium cheer your name and what it feels like to have a conference championship ring on your finger.

He knows all that, even though his official NFL career lists just two games played. But what a glorious night it was in one of them. That night was Monday, October 12, 1987—at Mile High Stadium.

A replacement player for the Denver Broncos during the 1987 NFL players' strike, Dudek ran for 128 yards and two touchdowns in a 30–14 victory over the Los Angeles Raiders.

Howie Long had trouble stopping him. Al Davis cursed him. And ABC's Frank Gifford praised him in front of a national television audience. How many people can say that?

"For one week, I knew what it was like to be John Elway in Denver," Dudek said. "People recognized me in restaurants and patted me on the back. I'll always take pride in that game and the other one we won [against Kansas City] for the Broncos. They counted in the standings, and without them, maybe we don't go to the Super Bowl like we did."

And it is that kind of memory that allows Dudek to smile fondly more than 20 years later. Following his short-lived NFL career, Dudek worked 50–60 hours a week for a beer distributor in

HERE, KID

The Broncos played Pittsburgh for the AFC championship in 2006 at Invesco Field at Mile High, having beaten the Steelers in the same game in the 1997–98 march to the Super Bowl.

A high school student in Pennsylvania named Joshua Vannoy went to school before the game dressed in the jersey of his all-time favorite player—John Elway. This didn't go over too well with one of his teachers, named John Kelly, who, shockingly, had Vannoy sit on the floor during a test and allowed other students to throw paper and spitballs at him.

Vannoy, understandably, couldn't concentrate on the test and did poorly. Kelly, a big Steelers fan, was unmoved. Vannoy was so bothered by the uproar of the incident, once it leaked to the public, that he transferred to another high school.

When Elway found out about it, he sent Vannoy a custom-made recliner. Only later in an investigation of the incident was it revealed that Kelly—who taught a class in ethnic relations—had a better-intentioned motive for his actions. Kelly wanted to teach his class what is was like for one person to be ganged up against by a mob, what prejudice really felt like. He kept his job.

Concord, New Hampshire, and then later as a sales manager in the same business in nearby Manchester. He's not bitter the Broncos cut him two weeks after his big Monday night performance. For him, there never was supposed to be any pro football anyway.

Dudek gained national prominence as a running back from Division III Plymouth State in New Hampshire when *Sports Illustrated* endorsed him for the 1985 Heisman Trophy. "What the heck, why not Dudek?" the cover read.

Some thought the cover appeared to be a joke, but his statistics were serious. In four years at Plymouth State, Dudek ran for 5,570 yards and an NCAA-record 79 touchdowns that finally was broken in 1994 by Carey Bender of Division III Coe College in Iowa (86 touchdowns). Dudek was a rock star in the small-time college football atmosphere of New Hampshire. True, it was just Division III football. But Dudek's speed was on par with Division I running backs, and he had an instinctive nose for the end zone.

"It was all just a blur there for a while," Dudek said. "I went on *Good Morning America* with Bo Jackson, played in the Japan Bowl, and a lot of other things. The hype was something." But nobody in the NFL seemed to care. Dudek went undrafted in 1986, and for a while he thought he would go to work as a carpenter in his native Quincy, Massachusetts. But he eventually was invited to the Broncos training camp as a free agent.

Broncos coach Dan Reeves liked his hustle and underdog spirit and signed Dudek to a contract. Before he could play in the regular season, however, Dudek hurt a shoulder and was put on injured reserve for the season. He was still a hit with Broncos fans.

"The fans in Denver were just the greatest," Dudek said. "I think they identified with me because I was an example of how anybody could make it. 1986 was a good year for me."

Dudek received a salary and an AFC championship ring, which he calls his "pride and joy," and went with the team to Super Bowl XXI in Pasadena, California.

The next season, Dudek was cut in camp. When the players went on strike, he resisted offers to become a "scab" when owners brought in replacement players.

Despite coming from a strong union family, Dudek eventually gave in and accepted Reeves's offer.

"I knew the system and they needed a lot of help in the running game," Dudek said. "I finally had to think of myself and what kind of opportunity it would be."

Dudek thought he had made the most of it with his Monday night performance, then caught five passes the next week at Kansas City. But when the strike was over, Dudek was cut again. Later attempts with Denver and the New York Jets failed. It was back to New Hampshire to work in the beer business, and for many years he worked for Coors, a mainstay corporation in Colorado.

"I always had a hard time gaining weight, although I don't have that problem now," Dudek said with a laugh. "I have no regrets, though. Those years in Denver were magic and I always looked at anything past Plymouth State to just be gravy, anyway.

"It's going to be real fun [with my] kids someday to sit down and tell them all about it."

THE THREE AMIGOS: THAT'S CATCHY

Want to laugh a little? Or, really hard? Punch in "Three Amigos" in the search bar on YouTube.com, and look for the video of Vance Johnson, Mark Jackson, and Ricky Nattiel on horseback.

Listen to the opening lyrics of the accompanying theme song:

In the city of the mile high.
the battle, it is drawing nigh
Let the Rocky Mountain Thunder roar...
send the Amigos off to war.

Watch as the Amigos emerge from a studio-produced hazy fog, clad in cowboy hats and coats, then yell *"Olé"* in tandem. Then, laugh.

It's easy to forget that at the height of their popularity, as receivers with the Broncos in the 1980s, Johnson, Jackson, and Nattiel were huge in Denver. All roughly the same size, all with roughly the same abilities as players, the trio was dubbed "the Three Amigos" and they weren't shy about marketing the name.

"The Amigos, touchdown Banditos."

The unquestioned height of their fame was prior to the 1988 Super Bowl, between Denver and the Washington Redskins. There were numerous features on them, including a long profile on the network pregame show. The hype did not seem overblown, not when John Elway threw a 56-yard touchdown strike to Nattiel on the Broncos' first play from scrimmage in the game.

TRIVIA

What Hall of Fame running back led the Broncos with 708 yards rushing in 1988?

Find the answers on pages 175–176.

VAN PELT'S CAREER HIGHLIGHT?

Bradlee Van Pelt did not play long for the Broncos—just three games at quarterback in 2005. But the former Colorado State Ram will long live as the answer to the trivia question, who completed the last pass to Jerry Rice? On September 2, 2005, in a preseason game at Arizona, Van Pelt completed a six-yard pass to the legendary receiver.

Rice hung up his cleats for good three days later.

"Olé," chimed the Three Amigos in the end zone.

Cue up the men with the potbellies in the mariachi band. Let them play their horns for the Three Amigos.

But, if you were a Denver Broncos fan at the moment of Nattiel's catch, you *believed* in the power of those lyrics.

Let the Rocky Mountain Thunder roar.
Send the Amigos off to war.
Ol' John in the shotgun,
puts the Redskins on the run
Bullets flying everywhere,
no one is safe with him out there!
You wanna say he'll take a chance,
deep to Ricky, Mark, or Vannnnnce!
40, 30, 20, 10,
Amigos they will strike again!
And you will hear the war cry,
echo down from fans on high....
"Hey! I know those guys!"

By the start of the 1989 season, everyone in Denver knew those guys. Jackson, the Chicago native who averaged 16.2 yards per catch in his career with Denver, the New York Giants, and Indianapolis, was already famous in the Mile High City for his catch that capped "The Drive" in Cleveland two years before.

Johnson, from Trenton, New Jersey, probably was the fastest of the Three Amigos on the field, and the most colorful off the field. There wasn't a camera he didn't love, and he was a regular staple of the many Broncos Sunday night highlight shows that started to proliferate in Denver in the late '80s and early '90s. He was always available for a quote, capped by a laugh from his dimpled chin. But, more than that, he was probably Elway's favorite receiver in the years the Three Amigos played together (1987–92). He always seemed to be open for one of Elway's desperation heaves—witness his fourth-down catch against Houston that helped win a 1992 playoff game.

Nattiel, a first-round draft pick in 1987 from the University of Florida, was probably the least known member of the Three Amigos, but he made many memorable catches, not just the one against the Redskins. He was always a favorite of Elway's in short-yardage situations in the red zone, with very sure hands and more toughness on his feet after the catch than the other two.

TRIVIA

Who were the only two Broncos players besides John Elway to wear No. 7?

Find the answers on pages 175–176.

The Three Amigos gave many thrills to Broncos fans, but it wasn't always sweetness and light. Johnson was involved in a couple of off-field incidents that stained his image, including a domestic violence charge and a handgun possession violation. Nattiel left the Broncos in 1992, in a trade to Tampa Bay that was poorly received at the time but turned out well for Denver.

Jackson left the Broncos for the New York Giants in 1993 after a falling-out with Denver management, catching 58 passes for his old coach, Dan Reeves. Still, Jackson is beloved in Denver for his catch in Cleveland.

While the Three Amigos video may now be a source of laughter—even, at the time of its release, it was to many—they have passed on into a kind of pantheon of beloved, cherished figures in Broncos history. And, at the time, they were as feared as any receiver corps in NFL history. Not many teams have one very good receiver, but the Broncos of then had three.

Too bad for Elway his coach, Reeves, wasn't a play-action passing kind of guy. Ask the Duke of Denver what one of his big regrets is from his playing days and he readily admits it is that he wasn't allowed to throw to the Three Amigos as much as he wanted—especially in the late '80s.

The Three Amigos still make the occasional personal appearance together in Denver, and the events are always well attended by Broncos fans. Somewhere in the basement of many orange and blue fans are signed posters of the three, standing with their cowboy hats and coats on.

Just don't ask if they have the video, too.

STRANGE BUT TRUE PEOPLE, PLACES, AND THINGS

YOU'RE FIRED! OKAY, MAYBE NOT

Floyd Little has his name on the Ring of Fame at Invesco Field at Mile High, immortalized as one of the Broncos' greatest players. On November 24, 1968, Little was told to get off the field at Mile High Stadium by coach Lou Saban during a game with the Buffalo Bills. Told that he was, in effect, fired as a member of the Broncos.

By the end of the game, Little was the hero, the player who made the big catch in a 34–32 victory. Good thing Saban wasn't the Donald Trump of football then. Little might not have gotten another chance. In his second year in the NFL, already having a season in which he would average five yards per carry, Little had been having a fine game entering the final two minutes against Buffalo. He'd amassed 170 yards from scrimmage, including a 66-yard TD reception from quarterback Marlin Briscoe. Little was the team's best offensive player, the big, bright hope in the team's future.

But with the Broncos leading 31–29 against Saban's former team, Little fumbled the ball back to Buffalo. Little's foot hit a tough patch of turf and he lost his balance, losing the ball without being hit—partly because he was awkwardly trying to stay in bounds to run out the clock, per Saban's instructions.

Buffalo's George Saimes recovered the fumble and ran the ball back to the Broncos' 10, tackled by Little. Buffalo kicked a field goal, and it was 32–31 with 30 seconds left. Saban blew a gasket on

SHHHH! NO TALKING BY O-LINEMEN

In 1995, Broncos offensive linemen decided as a group not to talk to the media—ever. No matter the media outlet, no matter the occasion, no matter what: there was to be no offensive lineman quoted anywhere, anytime.

This drove the media nuts, of course, especially at first. But with 24-hour sports broadcasts the norm, it became a story in itself.

The rule was broken a few times over the years, though. Gary Zimmerman gave a few sound bites to reporters, especially when it was falsely reported in the Rocky Mountain News one year that he would retire. Mark Schlereth, who went on to become a star football analyst with ESPN, gave a few words on occasion, and center Tom Nalen was quoted in the newspaper of his hometown in Massachusetts one year.

All three paid fines in the team's "Kangaroo Court." The money went into a fund used for a team party at the end of the year.

Into the early and mid-2000s, no talking among Broncos offensive linemen had become a team tradition. Not even the offensive line coaches would talk—even during media day at the Super Bowl.

the sideline; there was one team he wanted to beat over any other, and it was his old team, the Bills. Right before Little's fumble, the Bills blocked a punt and scored a touchdown. Now this.

Back in those days, NFL and AFL teams could not just "take a knee" four straight times to run out the clock with a lead. They had to run an actual play or be subject to a delay-of-game penalty. So, Little was just doing his job, wrapping his arm tight around the ball, ready to go down with the slightest hit. The bad Mile High turf prevented that, but Saban wasn't in the mood for excuses.

An old-school, emotional man with a temper perhaps rivaled only by Little's in its ferocity, Saban told his best player to go home. As Little trudged back onto the field to receive the Bills kickoff, Saban stormed up to him and said, "Get the hell out of here, you're fired!" Little assumed it was a bad joke, but Saban followed that up, according to Little's memoirs, with, "I'm serious.

You're fired. Highway 25 runs north and south, 70 east and west. Take your pick out of town."

"Screw you," said Little, who never backed down from a fight. But Little did walk off the field, furious. Never would he play for the Broncos—or certainly not Saban—ever again, he thought. Plenty of teams would want him anyway. Screw Saban, screw the Broncos. Little headed into the tunnel, toward the Broncos' locker room. But Little's huge pride got in the way. No way would he be bullied off the field over an honest mistake. He turned around and ran back toward the field.

By then, Saban had replaced Little with Fran Lynch, Little's roommate and backup at running back.

Little ran into the huddle and told Lynch to get back to the sideline. A game of chicken ensued, with Saban screaming at Little to get off the field and onto the highway, and Little refusing to budge. Referees demanded quick action, or a 12-men-on-the-field penalty would be assessed. Little would have to be physically removed—and it would have to be by someone a lot bigger and tougher than Saban. Finally, Lynch relented, tossing his arms in the air in frustration. He got chewed out by Saban for disobeying his orders to stay on the field. Little screamed profanities back at Saban. It was chaos. If that happened in today's modern sports era, it would have been replayed 10,000 times on *SportsCenter* and YouTube. It would have been grist for the talking-head, sports TV debate shows for days, weeks maybe.

DID YOU KNOW...

That longtime star running back Floyd Little was classified as a "homicidal maniac" by a personality test?

Early in his career, Little, like many Broncos players, was given such a test by coach Lou Saban. According to the results, Saban said, Little had the same psychological makeup of a homicidal maniac. Far from displeasing Saban, though, it made him appreciate Little's win-at-all-costs spirit that much more.

BY THE NUMBERS

$46,100—The amount of the final bid on eBay for the barrel worn by legendary Broncos superfan "Barrel Man" (also known as Tim McKernan) in 2006. The barrel was autographed by members of the Broncos' 1998 Super Bowl winning team.

Instead, it all ended happily ever after. Little told QB Briscoe to air it out to him, that he was going deep and would find a way to get open and catch the football. That's just what happened. Little ran a fly pattern and caught a 59-yard strike from Briscoe, on a play that started from the Denver 31 with 25 seconds left. Compounding matters for Buffalo, Buffalo was assessed a facemask penalty, putting Denver within field-goal range. One play later, Bobby Howfield had kicked a field goal and the Broncos were winners, 34–32. The crowd, as the cliché goes, went wild. Broncos players tossed their helmets in the air. Not Floyd Little, however. He sat on the bench, his head buried in his hands, crying. Always an emotional player, Little had trouble processing what had just happened. He'd gone from being a valued player to being told he was fired to being a hero, all in about two minutes.

Saban approached Little, but he was told in a most profane way to get lost. Little headed back into the same tunnel he'd thought he'd walked through for the last time minutes before. Saban called for him again, and this time Little screamed, "What the hell do you want?" "You've got one more week," Saban said, with a sheepish smile. Little had 295 total yards in the game—a Broncos record that stood for nearly three decades. A record game, from which he was fired by his head coach.

RICH KARLIS: "WOULDN'T THAT HURT?"

Rich Karlis still hears the question all the time: didn't it hurt to kick a football barefoot?

"Once I kind of got conditioned to it, it wasn't too bad," said Karlis, who served as Broncos place-kicker from 1982 to 1988.

"Practice or pregames when it was cold and snowy, it was a problem. But in a game, it wasn't a problem. It was only one kick." Karlis, today a marketing executive with Qwest Communications in Denver, is the last kicker in NFL history to kick barefoot full time, hanging up his one cleat for good in 1991.

The advent of lighter, more form-fitting shoes gradually phased out the barefoot kicker. But in Karlis's day, they were a presence. Five of the league's 28 kickers for a time in the 1980s kicked barefoot, and many in the college ranks did as well.

When kicking in the NFL evolved from the straight-ahead, toe-first style of its early years to a side-winding, "soccer style" in the 1970s and '80s, some kickers felt having no shoe gave them more direct control of the football. A ball traveled farther after hitting the naked bone at the top of a foot, the theory went, than being absorbed by a spongy shoe and cushy sock.

TRIVIA

Who is the only Broncos player, as of 2006, to have a last name beginning with the letter Q?

Find the answers on pages 175–176.

Tony Franklin became the first barefoot kicker in NFL history with the Philadelphia Eagles in 1979. After a failed stint as a punter with the University of Cincinnati, Karlis, who didn't even play football until his senior year in high school, gave barefoot place-kicking a try.

He found that kicking the oblong pigskin without a shoe came naturally, and he excelled enough to make the Broncos select him in 1982. Of all the kickers who went barefoot, which included Franklin, Mike Lansford, Paul McFadden, and Dave Warnke, Karlis naturally was asked the most about how much it hurt because of where he played. Many times on nationally televised games, Karlis trudged onto the field at Mile High Stadium on one of Denver's many freezing winter Sundays. With shots of Broncos fans bundled up from the bitter cold, out came Karlis looking like he was walking onto a Maui beach, ready to dip his toes in the water.

Didn't it feel like kicking a rock, kicking a hard football with a bare foot in sometimes single-digit temperatures?

Barefooted Rich Karlis follows through on his overtime field goal that gave the Broncos a 23–20 victory over the Cleveland Browns for the AFC championship in Cleveland on January 11, 1987.

NOT QUITE, COACH

John Ralston loved the communal, "Let's-go-get-'em, rah-rah" aspects of football. But in the NFL, it made more than a few of his Broncos players blanch.

One thing Ralston loved to do was run out onto the field before an opening kickoff and exhort his players.

"He'd come running on and say stuff like, 'We owe it to every one of these fans out there to give it our all' and 'There isn't an empty seat in the stadium today. Let's show 'em what we're made of.' That kind of stuff," said kicker Jim Turner.

"Well, one day he came on and Fran Lynch was on the field, and Fran was just one of the funniest guys. John came out and said his usual stuff, about every seat being filled, let's show 'em, and Fran just said with a real deadpan voice, 'Uh, coach, I see a seat empty up there' and he pointed at it. We all cracked up in the huddle and John just ran off the field with his tail between his legs."

"When you hit the football right, not really," Karlis says. "It's like the baseball hitter, who connects with the ball in the 'sweet spot.' You didn't feel it, especially with the added element of adrenaline, kicking in front of 80,000 people."

Besides, Karlis had an insulated, thermal boot he wore on the sideline. Only for a few seconds at a time was Karlis actually on the field, barefoot.

Kickers naturally are considered "oddballs" by their NFL teammates, and Karlis's barefoot style made him seem like even more of an alien being to some of his Broncos mates. But far from being aloof, Karlis reveled in being "one of the boys," often hanging out with the biggest and rowdiest members of the team. He kept teammates in stitches with a dead-on impression of coach Dan Reeves, and he was known as a prankster.

Karlis was part of a band of players who regularly pulled fast ones on teammates; Karlis himself was the victim of several, such as having a garbage can full of water dumped on him from five stories every year by linebacker Randy Gradishar at training camp

in Greeley, Colorado, and sometimes seeing his one football shoe
hanging from a tree.

He remembers hulking lineman
and good friend, Keith Bishop,
getting back at a previous prank
from Gradishar by having a buddy
send him a live, five-foot bull snake
and dropping it into the bottom of Gradishar's laundry basket.

TRIVIA

What is the origin of the
name "Denver Broncos"?

Find the answers on pages 175–176.

"Gradishar hated snakes, and he jumped about 10 feet when
that thing came tumbling out," Karlis said.

Then there was the time receiver Steve Watson treated everybody to a bowl full of Milk Duds on the training camp training
table.

"We watched guys stuffing them down. But they weren't Milk
Duds. They were chocolate-covered elk turds," Karlis recalls with
a belly laugh.

For a person who never stepped foot—barefoot or not—onto
a football field until his last year of high school, Karlis had quite
a career in the game. To Broncos fans, he'll probably best be
known for kicking the winning, 34-yard field goal in overtime
against Cleveland in the 1987 AFC Championship Game.

But Karlis is also well remembered by fans of the Minnesota
Vikings, for kicking seven field goals in a 1989 game. Entering the
2006 season, that still qualified him as the coholder of the NFL
record. For several years, Karlis also held the record for the longest
field goal in Super Bowl history (48 yards, in 1987).

WANNA BUY A POOL TABLE?

John Elway was so competitive and hated to lose so much that, one day
after losing a game on his pool table at home, he sold it. Elway had never
lost to anyone on his table, until backup quarterback Bubby Brister beat him.
The table was gone the next day.

DID YOU KNOW...

That Broncos defensive lineman Rich "Tombstone" Jackson was responsible for a change to NFL rules?

Jackson was the first player to use a "head slap" technique to get to the quarterback. He was devastatingly effective in knocking offensive linemen off balance, or just right to the ground, with a single slap to the head. By the end of Jackson's career, the NFL Competition Committee made head slaps punishable by a penalty.

Karlis is not as fondly remembered by Broncos fans for missing two seeming chip-shot field-goal attempts in the 1987 Super Bowl against the New York Giants, but the kick in Cleveland, his several solid seasons of service to the Broncos, and a continued presence in the Denver community with several charitable ventures make Karlis still a popular figure to Broncos fans today.

"I still am amazed at how much the Broncos mean to this community," Karlis said. "You meet people all the time who remember every little thing from the time I played. Some of them have tears in their eyes when they talk about how much those teams meant to them, and still do. My life was so charmed. I got to play in the NFL, I got to play in Denver—probably one of the top places you could want to play in the NFL if you could."

When Karlis tied the field-goal record with his seven for Minnesota, Karlis—lacking a shoe to give it—had a plaster cast of his right foot made and sent to the Pro Football Hall of Fame. For a kid who grew up in Salem, Ohio, having anything from his career reside in the hallowed halls of nearby Canton is an unequaled thrill.

"Like I said, my life was charmed," he said.

THE MARK SCHLERETH THEME SONG: "CUTS LIKE A KNIFE"

Mark Schlereth has had his body operated on 29 times. Do not contact the publisher of this book, pointing out a typo by the author. He really has. And he's still a young guy. That's a lot of knives, a lot of anesthesia.

"Maybe that explains a few things," says the funny, outgoing native of Anchorage, Alaska, who today is a popular football analyst on ESPN.

Twenty of Schlereth's first 29 surgeries were to his knees, fifteen on the left, five on the right. One of his first surgeries was in 1985, for a torn anterior cruciate ligament.

"It was archaic when you look back to how they did them, even then, which wasn't that long ago," Schlereth said. "Surgeries are just so less invasive now than they used to be."

The number of times Schlereth has gone under the knife shows what a competitor and how tough he was. In 2000, after surgery number 13 on his left knee, Broncos coach Mike Shanahan said doctors told him it was the worst knee injury they'd ever seen. But he went on to play two more productive seasons for the Broncos before retiring in 2001. By then, he'd won three Super Bowl rings, played in a Pro Bowl, and firmly established himself as the most favored son of the American Medical Association.

On the day of his retirement announcement, April 18, 2001, Schlereth showed that he might have a future in TV: "The reason I came out here today was to announce that I have just signed a six-year, $42 million contract to extend my career with the Denver Broncos," he told reporters. "The truth of the matter is,

WHO ARE YOU?

On a night before the Broncos' first Super Bowl, in New Orleans, third-string quarterback Craig Penrose went down to Bourbon Street for some fun with teammate John Grant.

The two NFL players, about to play in the biggest football game in the world, went totally unrecognized at a couple of hot spots—even by their own fans. "There were Too Tall Jones and Tom Henderson all dressed up and getting the attention," Penrose told *The Denver Post* at the time. "We could walk right past them and nobody said anything."

Howard Griffith follows lineman Mark Schlereth into the end zone to score Denver's first touchdown of Super Bowl XXXIII against the Atlanta Falcons. Schlereth sacrificed a lot for his football career—29 surgeries, to be exact— but he came away with three Super Bowl rings.

after going through my 15th operation on my left knee last November, it became painfully obvious that I couldn't sign a six-year contract for $42 worth of Tupperware. I started to realize in the last three months of free agency that there is not a lot of market for a 6'3", 245-pound guard that is 35 years old and beat to a pulp."

TRIVIA

What was the coldest game played in Mile High Stadium history?

Find the answers on pages 175–176.

Schlereth was never supposed to amount to much in the NFL, at least according to the scouts, but he had one of the finest careers an offensive lineman could ever have. While he was a big man by society's standards, he was considered small by those of the NFL for offensive linemen. Two hundred and forty-five pounds is considered pip-squeak size for linemen in today's NFL.

Schlereth came out of the University of Idaho as the 263rd pick, by Washington, in the 1989 NFL Draft. With the Vandals, Schlereth blocked for quarterback John Friesz, who would go on to the NFL. Still, Schlereth was considered just too small to be able to make it in the NFL.

But Schlereth was smart and always wanted to learn new techniques. His biggest asset was his incredible work ethic.

"I always told myself, 'I'll outwork everybody,'" he said. "I just made a pact with myself that nobody would ever outwork me. I'm proud of that. I think I kept that pact."

Schlereth was a popular teammate, known for a few practical jokes or cutting barbs. When he came to the Broncos as a free

WHAT A ROMANTIC

When he was a student at Stanford, John Elway went on a date with a lithesome Cardinal swimmer named Janet Buchan. On their first date, Elway played catch with a football with Buchan—and broke her finger with a pass. That didn't dissuade her from marrying him a year later.

GREEN BEANS! NO, PEAS!

How out of control did the media coverage of John Elway get in his rookie year? Consider: An actual sniping contest between Denver's two daily newspapers, the *Post* and the *Rocky Mountain News*, started over what Elway ate for dinner one night in training camp. One paper reported that Elway ate fried chicken and peas for dinner. The other paper said it was fried chicken and green beans. This became a real, honest-to-goodness dispute among the knights of the keyboard!

agent in 1995, after six strong years with the Redskins, he acquired the nickname "Stink." One day, he told some teammates about a job his sister used to have at a restaurant in Alaska— cutting off the heads of fish and serving them as a delicacy, known as "stinkheads." Pretty soon, he was known around the locker room as Stink.

Schlereth is yet another ex-Bronco you could make a case for deserving Pro Football Hall of Fame induction. Maybe not a huge case, but consider: Not many players ever won three Super Bowls, and Schlereth was a main blocker for a running back (Terrell Davis) that had one of the top five rushing seasons in NFL history, and for some of the highest-scoring offenses in league history. He played 12 years, which is a long career by NFL standards, and, despite the incredible number of surgeries, he didn't miss too many games.

Schlereth was lucky he didn't play in the 1950s, '60s, and '70s. Indeed, surgeries in those days usually involved a complete flaying back of the skin and muscle tissue. Take a look at the knees of some old NFL stars, such as Joe Namath, Jim Otto, Conrad Dobler, and many others, and one sees something akin to a child's Etch-a-Sketch drawing: long, deep scars from surgical cuts, criss-crossing each other.

Although Schlereth is believed to have undergone the most surgeries of any NFL player ever, he was able to walk away from the game in the literal sense—although it will never be a pain-free rest of his life.

"It's something you just learn to live with. There's always going to be some pain, but you deal with it," Schlereth says. "I know I gave everything I had to my football career, my teammates, and my coaches. I was really blessed to play for the teams I did, with the players I did, and the coaches I played for. Yeah, there was some pain involved, but I would never trade any of it. Pain makes you stronger."

In fact, Schlereth keeps many of the bone fragments from his surgeries in a jar, as a reminder of that pain.

Schlereth went on to a highly successful career in the media, becoming one of ESPN's most frequent and popular football analysts.

TRIVIA

For many years, the Broncos had a fan named "Barrel Man," who wore nothing but an orange barrel around his waist, with cowboy boots and hat. Barrel Man's real name was Tim McKernan. What was his occupation in real life?

Find the answers on pages 175–176.

He also pitched how-to videos for prospective linemen on his own website—www.markschlereth.com—and is writing a book geared toward women of all ages about how they can survive living with male football junkies. One of Schlereth's children, daughter Alexandria, became a successful actress on the television show *Desire*.

Schlereth made part of his post-playing-career living with words despite the fact he couldn't read until age seven, having been dyslexic. It was just another one of the obstacles Schlereth overcame and outworked.

ELWAY'S BOYHOOD HERO

Despite growing up in California, with some closer NFL teams and players nearby, John Elway's favorite player as a kid was one from the Dallas Cowboys. Elway idolized Cowboys running back Calvin Hill, to the point where he wore his number in youth football and called himself Calvin Elway.

THE MEN IN CHARGE

PAT BOWLEN: LOVE HIM? OR HATE HIM?

Pat Bowlen looks like a guy who would be easy to dislike. He is rich and grew up rich. He has a beautiful, blond wife, Annabel. He is a top triathlete, even into his sixties. He is always tan. He prowled the Broncos sidelines in his early years as owner dressed in a fur coat. And he has a natural look on his face that seems a little, well, arrogant.

Many people did dislike Bowlen over the years, for some of the aforementioned reasons. Then there was the issue of Invesco Field at Mile High—which was built largely through a sales tax increase from the public, with Bowlen "crying poverty" in the words of some of his most ardent critics.

Bowlen may not be loved by everybody, but nobody can deny he's been a big success in life. He and his family bought the Broncos from Edgar Kaiser for $78 million on March 23, 1984, becoming majority owners and 100 percent owners by 1985. By 2004, according to *Forbes* magazine, the Broncos were worth $815 million and played in a stadium whose $401 million price tag was funded 75 percent by taxpayers.

So, Pat Bowlen is certainly no dummy. Although he has a reputation—as do many NFL owners—of being a ruthless businessman, the native of Prairie du Chien, Wisconsin, has a softer side that many don't know about.

Since 1993, when he established the Denver Broncos Charities Fund, Bowlen and his team have given nearly $30 million to the underprivileged. He was the chairman of the Colorado Special Olympics for 19 years. Bowlen never was just a big check writer, either; he put in countless hours with handicapped kids, making sure they were taken care of as best he and his organizations could provide.

TRIVIA

Where did the Broncos hold their first training camp, in 1960?

Find the answers on pages 175–176.

"To me, he's the best owner in pro sports," says former Broncos kicker Jim Turner. "He's done an awful lot for the community. He's given millions of dollars and lots of his time to good causes, and he's given fans of the Broncos a chance to see a winner every year, always trying to build a champion."

Another hidden fact about Bowlen is his appreciation for the players who helped make him rich as an NFL owner. The Broncos did not have much of an alumni program when Bowlen first bought the team, with not one former player serving with the team in any capacity. Not only did Bowlen put many ex-players to work in community relations, but he also established the Ring of Fame at Mile High Stadium. Many Broncos fans probably would have no idea who Goose Gonsoulin was, or Frank Tripucka, if not for seeing their names lining the stadium every Sunday.

Bowlen did things like pay all the funeral expenses for cornerback Darrent Williams—along with the cost of flying the entire team to Fort Worth, Texas, to attend the funeral—in 2007. He also offered a $100,000 reward for information leading to the conviction of Williams's killer.

Those are some of the good things about Bowlen, but many people in Denver still resent how he built Invesco Field at Mile High. They felt he used the team's Super Bowl success in 1997–98 to force an early election to decide whether the stadium would receive taxpayer funding. There was probably much truth to that, but it showed Bowlen's shrewd business nature. He had

Owner Pat Bowlen has been the clear authority figure for the Broncos since he and his family bought the franchise in 1984.

the leverage at the time, and he used it to his advantage. The Broncos were defending champions and undefeated when the stadium election was held in November 1998. Opponents of the measure favored by Bowlen never had a chance.

One other thing that set Bowlen apart from many owners in pro sports was his ability to stay calm in the face of adversity or dissenting public opinion. Many owners have fired coaches too soon over the years (Al Davis with Mike Shanahan in Oakland, for starters) or traded good players away after one bad year—only to have them return to haunt their teams.

The Broncos have had few such mistakes in the Bowlen era. From 1984 to 2007, the Broncos had just three head coaches under Bowlen (Dan Reeves, Wade Phillips, and Shanahan). There have been few bad trades—and can you imagine how Bowlen would be remembered today by Broncos fans if he had bowed to public pressure and traded John Elway to the Washington Redskins in the early 1990s, as came close to happening? Bowlen always had the ability to say, in effect, "Let's cool our jets here and not do anything too rash."

That paid off in Elway winning two Super Bowls. Bowlen's patience paid off again with Shanahan becoming one of the NFL's all-time top winning coaches—after many people thought he was no more than top-assistant material, not a head coach.

Bowlen, whose father made it big as a wildcatter in the Canadian Northwest oil business, also made a fortune in oil before buying the Broncos. He also is a member of the bar in Alberta, Canada.

More than anything to do with oil or law, however, Bowlen will always be known as the first owner to bring the Broncos a Super Bowl title. His lifting the Vince Lombardi Trophy in San Diego after Super Bowl XXXII and telling the world "This one's for John" will always bring a smile to the faces of Broncos fans.

The smiles brought to the faces of thousands of underprivileged kids, much of it from Bowlen's time and money, may not be known to the world like his salute to Elway. But to the people who know Bowlen well—and there aren't too many—those smiles will be better remembered for the man who inspired them.

DAN REEVES: DON'T TREAD ON ME

A terrific way to get a lively sports bar conversation going—particularly one in an older neighborhood—is to throw out the question, was Dan Reeves a great coach or not in his time with the Broncos?

For the affirmative, the argument would go like this: Dan Reeves posted a 110–73–1 record with the Broncos, from 1981 to 1992, and led the Broncos to three AFC championships.

For the negative, it would go like this: Dan Reeves had a 7–6 playoff record in Denver, and all three of his Super Bowl teams were blown out.

There is validity to both arguments. What can't be argued is that Reeves did enjoy a level of success previously never achieved by a Broncos head coach. His victory total ranks second in team

John Elway celebrates a fourth-quarter touchdown against the Atlanta Falcons as the Broncos finally broke through for a win in Super Bowl XXXIII on January 31, 1999.

history, and he is one of only a handful of coaches to take two different teams to a Super Bowl.

That championship ring always eluded him as a coach, however. To his detractors, Reeves's loss to the Broncos in Super Bowl XXXIII as coach of the Falcons—with John Elway the MVP—was sweet justice for the way he screwed up the Hall of Fame quarterback for so many years with his dumbed-down play calling and controlling personality.

Thankfully, the feud that once existed between Reeves and Elway—which led Elway to call their time together "hell" and for Reeves to respond that it wasn't "heaven" for him either—was put behind them.

When Elway was elected to the Pro Football Hall of Fame in 2004, he invited Reeves to the ceremony in Canton, Ohio.

"I owe Dan a big thank you," Elway said in his acceptance speech. "He was another of those pillars of my career that if it wasn't for him, chances are I wouldn't be standing here."

Reeves always had a quick temper, but he was even quicker to forgive and forget. He said the invitation from Elway was "one of the greatest things that ever happened to me" and the two are friends today.

It wasn't always that way, of course. Elway chafed at Reeves's conservative play calling, and Reeves just plain chafed at anyone questioning his authority. But it was more than that.

Reeves came from the Deep South—he might have the thickest southern accent in NFL history—and grew up poor, with a couple of major illnesses. He was undrafted by the NFL but fought his way onto the roster of the Dallas Cowboys as a running back and was a solid contributor to several excellent teams, including the 1971 Super Bowl winners.

Elway was the golden child, the California kid with the surfer's hair and rifle arm. Everything seemed to come easy for him—too easy, perhaps, for a guy like Dan Reeves.

As outwardly different as they were, and as different as their backgrounds were, Reeves and Elway were exactly alike in one big way: they burned to win. Both men could be stubborn and think their way was the best way, and so it was natural they would clash many times.

Cameras often caught Reeves and Elway barking at one another on the sideline following a bad play. Until 1993, when the "heaven and hell" comments were made, they rarely sniped at each other in the press. But it was an open secret in the Denver media that the two often hated each other. Former *Denver Post* columnist Dick Connor was the first to go public, in 1990, with news of a rift between the two. Elway told Connor, "We hardly talk to each other unless it's game time."

When Reeves was fired by the Broncos and landed with the New York Giants, the feud busted wide open in the papers, and Elway later criticized Reeves's coaching with the Giants, pointing out that the Giants were last in NFL offense under Reeves and that he didn't "change with the game."

If only the Broncos could have won one of the three Super Bowls in which Reeves coached Elway, no feud likely would have existed. Then again, maybe it would have. Terry Bradshaw and

While fans might debate his greatness as a coach during his time in Denver, Dan Reeves was an enduring influence on the players he coached.

Chuck Noll won four Super Bowls together in Pittsburgh, but they almost never got along. Phil Simms hated his championship coach, Bill Parcells, at times. Jim McMahon and Mike Ditka didn't always get along, and neither did Don Shula and Dan Marino.

The Super Bowl losses did exacerbate Reeves's and Elway's tense relationship, however. Elway believed a more "West Coast" offense—in which he could throw more passes to a greater variety of receivers—would put the Broncos over the top. Reeves favored a more conservative, clock-control approach. Even after the feel-good days of "The Drive" in Cleveland and the tough-but-honorable first Super Bowl loss to the Giants, bad feelings were starting to fester.

TRIVIA

What former Los Angeles Rams star quarterback was the Broncos' QB and receivers coach in 1983, John Elway's first year in the NFL?

Find the answers on pages 175–176.

"It was *Mutiny on the Bounty*," Broncos cornerback Louis Wright said, in *John Elway: Armed and Dangerous*. "The players believed Dan was becoming a dictator.... The players were saying, 'Hey, if it's going to be another year of this, then we're going to have to get Dan out of here. If we have to lose every game, then we're going to lose every game.' The players kept saying 'somebody had to tell him,' and the players said, 'Louie, you're the player rep.'"

Wright did talk to Reeves, who did not take it well. In 1987, Wright retired from the Broncos, despite seeming to have several more good years left in him. Elway and Reeves coexisted another few years, but everything fell apart in 1992. Reeves fired Elway's confidant, quarterbacks coach Mike Shanahan, for alleged insubordination. Former Patriots coach and Baltimore Colts Hall of Fame receiver Raymond Berry was brought in to replace Shanahan—but what was a receiver doing coaching the QBs? Elway and others wanted to know.

After an 8–8 season in 1992, Broncos owner Pat Bowlen fired Reeves and replaced him with Wade Phillips. For a while after the dismissal, Reeves had bragging rights over Elway, Bowlen, and the

Broncos; his new team, the Giants, went 11–5 in 1993 and won a game in the playoffs, and he was named NFL Coach of the Year. The Broncos stumbled to a 9–7 season and backed into the playoffs, getting crushed by the Raiders in a wild-card game.

Elway, of course, got the last laugh. But by the time Elway was the MVP in a Super Bowl win over Reeves's Falcons—and especially when their active NFL days ended—the pettiness between the two men had been replaced by reflective maturity. Their relationship was like a marriage: it had its ups and downs, but in the final analysis, a lot of good came from it and both learned a lot of valuable lessons.

MIKE SHANAHAN: MASTER (MIND) AND COMMANDER

In 1994, Mike Shanahan was a man who had been to four Super Bowls as a coach, winning one as offensive coordinator of the San Francisco 49ers that year. But none of the Super Bowl appearances came with Shanahan as a head coach, and in 1994 the native of Illinois had a career NFL record of 8–12 as a head guy.

Five years later, Shanahan had two world championship rings as head coach of the Broncos and, aside from owner Pat Bowlen, was the most powerful man in the organization.

"Denver is a place that, obviously, I'll always have a special feeling for," Shanahan said. "So many great things have happened here, for myself and my family. It's been wonderful."

It wasn't a totally smooth ride to the top for Shanahan. Far from it. He was head coach of the Los Angeles Raiders in 1988 and for four games in 1989. Shanahan was fired by Raiders boss Al Davis, with the team's record 1–3. Shanahan was bitter for a while over the firing—especially over a financial issue: Shanahan said he was stiffed on part of his salary by Davis. But he was too much of a go-getter to remain out of work for long, and he returned to the Broncos as a quarterbacks coach. Before getting the Raiders job, Shanahan had been offensive coordinator of the Broncos for three years, and he had a good relationship with Bowlen and, maybe more important, with quarterback John Elway.

A former quarterback himself at East Leyden High School in Franklin Park, Illinois, and at Eastern Illinois University, Shanahan

Long considered one of the brightest minds in football, Mike Shanahan has validated those accolades time and again with two Super Bowls and many successful seasons since he was named coach of the Broncos in 1995.

loved the offensive part of football. He had a fertile mind for offensive schemes and was a disciple of legendary 49ers coach Bill Walsh, particularly his "scripted" first 10- or 15-play strategy. Shanahan dreamed of a life as a pro QB, but he was too small and injury-prone. At Eastern Illinois, in fact, he almost died from a football injury. Shanahan urinated blood at one point following a hit during a game with the Panthers, but avoided the hospital until it was almost too late.

"My heart stopped beating for more than 30 seconds," Shanahan told *Sports Illustrated* in 1997. "A priest read me my last rites. My dad got to the hospital as the priest was walking out." Shanahan recovered and immediately resumed his type-A lifestyle, even going river rafting a few weeks later. Into his late fifties, Shanahan hadn't changed. He was the usual workaholic football coach, but Shanahan always took things to extremes. He rarely slept more than a few hours a night, always watching film, always scheming to find new ways to win games.

He won a lot of them in Denver, and by 2004, he had become just one of four coaches in the history of the NFL to spend 10 or more years consecutively as head coach with one team. He also was the team's executive vice president of football operations—which meant that he was in control of just about everything, even though Ted Sundquist held the title of general manager for years. Sundquist's title shouldn't have fooled anybody, however; Shanahan was the man really in charge of things personnel-wise.

In Denver's back-to-back Super Bowl–winning years in the late '90s, Shanahan was dubbed the "Mastermind" by the media. Winning lends itself to such nicknames, of course. But partly it was given because of Shanahan's obsession with scripting a football game to just his specifications, especially offensively.

And yet, the nickname would come to be questioned by many in the same media years later. Was Shanahan really a "mastermind," people asked, after the Broncos failed to win a playoff game from 2000 to 2005, following the retirement of Elway. Was Shanahan really a mastermind for believing that Brian Griese could effectively lead the Broncos as a QB after Elway?

For sure, Shanahan had some critics, even after the Super Bowl years, but here are the facts:

- From 1995 to 2005, no coach in the NFL had a better record than Shanahan's 114–62 (.648).
- Only two other coaches (Bill Belichick and Don Shula) won two Super Bowls as fast with one team as Shanahan, who won it all in his third and fourth years on the job.

- Two of the offenses he was associated with (San Francisco, 1994, and Denver, 1998) were among the six highest-scoring teams in league history. The 49ers' 636 total points (regular season and playoffs) in '94 remains the NFL record.

Shanahan could be prickly at times, like most coaches, but he was known for his cool on and off the field. He did not blow up at the media like many have done—from Woody Hayes to Vince Lombardi to Dennis Green—and often poked fun at his serious persona. Shanahan's response after losses was almost always the same: "We didn't get the job done."

He could be tough on players, and he rubbed some fans the wrong way for cutting loose some popular stars, such as Shannon Sharpe, Trevor Pryce, Ashley Lelie, and Steve Atwater, among others. He also nearly left the Broncos in 2002 for the University of Florida.

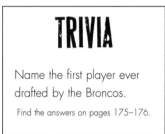

TRIVIA

Name the first player ever drafted by the Broncos.

Find the answers on pages 175–176.

Shanahan met with Gators officials in Denver, creating a media circus. But in the end, Bowlen talked him into staying—helped along by a healthy raise and beefed-up job title.

Shanahan failed to win a Super Bowl in the eight years following Elway's retirement, winning just one playoff game in five appearances. But, entering the 2007 season, Shanahan was still firmly in charge of the Broncos, with no letup in sight. And no matter what happened from there, nobody would ever be able to take away the fact that the first time the Broncos ever lifted the Vince Lombardi Trophy, Shanahan was the head coach.

While teams like the Raiders crumbled, Shanahan had his Broncos teams consistently in the postseason hunt, having just one losing season (6–10 in 1999) his first 13 years on the job. By any definition, such a record qualifies Shanahan as deserving the nickname of "winner."

ANSWERS

Page 8: Denver beat the Pittsburgh Steelers 34–21 at Mile High Stadium in an AFC playoff game on December 24, 1977 . It was also the first playoff game ever played by the Broncos.

Page 13: Denver had the NFL's top rushing defense in 1977, 1979, and 1996. From 1960 to 2006, the Broncos never had a number one passing defense, nor a number one overall defense.

Page 14: The only season the Broncos finished number one in total NFL offense is 1996.

Page 25: Tom Jackson and Dennis Smith both played 14 years in a Broncos uniform, Jackson from 1973 to 1986 and Smith from 1981 to 1994.

Page 30: Floyd Little, Rich Jackson, Lionel Taylor, and Goose Gonsoulin are the first four players in the Ring of Fame.

Page 64: On January 2, 1994, the Broncos had a comfortable 30–13 lead over the Los Angeles Raiders, with 10:31 left in the third quarter at the L.A. Coliseum. The Raiders scored the game's last 20 points, winning 33–30 in overtime.

Page 93: In Super Bowl XXI, in Pasadena, California, 101,063 saw the Broncos lose to the New York Giants.

Page 96: On September 23, 1984, Chris Norman had an 83-yard punt for the Broncos against Kansas City at Mile High Stadium. Incidentally, the longest punt in NFL history—98 yards, by Steve O'Neal of the New York Jets in 1969—came against the Broncos.

Page 144: Tony Dorsett played the final year of his Hall of Fame, 12-year career for the Broncos in 1988, wearing the familiar No. 33 he donned for so many years with the Dallas Cowboys.

Page 146: Mickey Slaughter (1963–66) and Craig Morton (1977–82) both wore No. 7.

Page 152: Running back Frank Quayle, who played 11 games for the Broncos in 1969, is the only player with a last name beginning with Q.

Page 155: The name "Denver Broncos" was chosen from 500 entries in a name-the-team contest in January 1960. The name was suggested by Ward M. Vining of Lakewood, Colorado. But the football team isn't the first Denver Broncos in the city's sports history. Denver's 1921 entry in the Midwest Baseball League was also called the Broncos.

Page 159: On December 10, 1972, the thermometer at game time read just 9 degrees Fahrenheit at Mile High Stadium, for a game against San Diego. It should be pointed out, however, that many games from 1960 to 1969 did not include official temperatures at the opening kickoff. The coldest game the Broncos ever played on the road was on December 18, 1983, in Kansas City, where the temperature was zero and the wind chill factor was minus 30.

Page 161: Tim "Barrel Man" McKernan was a mechanic for United Airlines.

Page 163: The Broncos held their first training camp at the Colorado School of Mines, in Golden. Other training camp sites over the years include Colorado State University (1962–64, 1976–81), Adams County, Colorado (1967–71), California Poly-Pomona (1972–75), University of Northern Colorado (1982–2002), and the current Paul D. Bowlen Memorial Broncos Centre, in Englewood.

Page 169: John Hadl was quarterback and receivers coach in 1983.

Page 173: Roger LeClerc, a kicker/linebacker from Trinity, in Connecticut, was Denver's first selection in the inaugural American Football League draft, November 22, 1959. LeClerc was also drafted by the Chicago Bears of the NFL, however, and began his career in Chicago. He played eight games for the Broncos in 1967.